Sex & Lies & Vast Conspiracies

by David Horowitz

Second Thoughts Books is an imprint of the Center for the Study of Popular Culture, P.O. Box 67398, Los Angeles, CA 90067, (800) 752-6562.

ISBN: 1-886442-14-2

Printed in the United States of America
2 3 4 5 6 7 8 9 10

Contents

L et the reader beware. What follows is a series of dispatches from the cultural battlefront rather than a book in the usual sense. The columns and articles that make up this volume reflect on the unfolding crisis of the Clinton presidency and the ideological currents that lie behind it.

Though rarely acknowledged outside the reaches of the political right, the causes of this crisis are clear enough: Disrespect for morality, disrespect for family, disrespect for institutional authority, disrespect for the White House, disrespect for America itself. The Clinton scandal derisively known as "Zippergate" is at its root a Sixties affair. The Administration may not be Camelot (more like Dogpatch, as my partner Peter Collier has quipped) but the agony of the Clinton presidency is unmistakably a crisis created by the long-running assault on this nation and its institutions by the political generation of Hillary and Bill.

This assault includes the creation of the special prosecutor's office and the Watergate hearings, whose real purpose was to criminalize political differences and to achieve the retreat from Vietnam that liberals had failed to secure at the polls. It was carried on through more than 25 congressional investigations and special prosecutions instigated by Democratic legislators during the Reagan-Bush years when congress was firmly in control of the left. It assumed a new dimension with the feminist-driven campaign to deprive Clarence Thomas of a seat on the Supreme Court in the summer of 1991, which has direct bearing on the legal problems that have derailed the Clinton presidency. With liberal defenders of Clinton now steadfastly maintaining that his Oval Office seduction of twenty-one-year-old intern Monica Lewinsky is a "private" and non-culpable act, it is strange to recall how the same people almost succeeded in depriving Thomas of a Supreme Court seat for allegedly engaging in off-color *talk* to a Yale lawyer named Anita Hill.

Indeed, the crisis of the Clinton presidency would not have been possible without the efforts of the left to criminalize political differences and the feminists' success in criminalizing sexual misbehavior. As writer Noemie Emery summarized: "No Anita Hill, no harassment culture. No harassment culture, no harassment law. No harassment law, no Paula Jones. No Paula Jones, no discovery process. No discovery process, no other women. No other women, no lies. No lies, no perjury charges, no witness tampering, no obstruction of justice, no crisis, no talk of removal. Anita Hill brought on the great Clinton crisis. The feminists laid the groundwork for the destruction of their own."†

The first metasticism of these radical developments in American moral and legal attitudes was the disgraceful witch-hunt of American war heroes over the infamous party after the "Tailhook" convention of 1991. The complaint of a disgruntled female naval lieutenant that she had been unwillingly groped after that party, triggered a national feminist hysteria that led to the termination of dozens of military careers and the purge of an officer corps to a degree unprecedented in American military annals. This witch-hunt was accompanied by much pious speechifying on the part of high government officials who declared that the national purpose demanded that military leaders learn to be "sensitive" to women. In light of the current presidential gropings and seductions, and the defense of this behavior by the same voices demanding those heads in the past, this concern now seems positively quaint.

The collected articles in this volume look at the conflicted state of America's political culture over the issues of race and sex, at a point in time when these disputes could lead the nation in several possible directions. It is my hope that this small volume will help to push them in the direction of greater public sanity.

With the exception of the article titled "Dialogue on Race," which appeared first in the *Los Angeles Times*, the shorter pieces in this book were written as columns for the Internet magazine *Salon* (www.salonmagazine.com) where my by-line appears every other Monday.

"Feminist Assault on the Military" was given as testimony before the President's Commission on the Assignment of Women in the Armed Forces, in the summer of 1992 during the presidential campaign that led to Clinton's first-term election.

Both "Tailhook Witch-hunt" and "Michael Lind and the Right-wing Cabal" first appeared in *Heterodoxy*.

"A Political Romance" was published in the *San Diego Union*.

"Up From Multiculturalism" was originally a talk given at the National Association of Scholars Annual Meeting in New Orleans, December 12-14, 1997.

"Character Assassination as a Political Weapon" appears here in print for the first time.

March 21, 1998

---

† "Hillary Clinton and the Crisis of Feminism," *The Weekly Standard*, March 9, 1998.

Monica Lewinsky

Bill Clinton

Gennifer Flowers

Hillary Rodham Clinton

Clintongate

It's Only Sex?

F rom every cyber-pulpit and satellite perch in the nation, the cry of the President's defenders goes forth: *It's only sex! It's none of your business! Leave him alone!*

Come again? Isn't this what the good old boys used to say in the bad old days when confronted with evidence of their sexual misconduct? Haven't we had our collective consciousness raised since then? Isn't everyone supposed to recognize now that disrespecting other human beings as sexual objects is—how shall we put it—socially incorrect? And what about the trashing of the victims, those self-exculpatory aggressions that always accompany such exposures? *She wanted it. She stalked him. She asked for it.* Don't these claims have an uncanny resemblance to current talking-points on the White House spin sheet in *les affaires* Lewinsky, Willey, and Jones?

Remember the old Watergate bumper stickers? The ones with the picture of Nixon saying "Would you buy a used car from this man?" Well, would you buy one from *this* president? Wasn't the point of the old question a serious one after all? The inability to trust the chief executive is necessarily a matter of state.

Consider the recent military minuet over the Persian Gulf. Is Saddam Hussein a Hitler threatening imminent genocide? Were all those war noises emanating from the White House really directed at Iraq? Or did they serve more personal Clinton agendas? And what about the outcome? Is the deal that bought the peace one we can really trust, or has the President merely (and momentarily) gotten *himself* off the hook—first by deflecting attention from his troubles and then by agreeing to a face-saving exit from a war he didn't want to fight? Are we really safer as result of our aborted campaign? Or is it only Bill Clinton who gained respite from *his* travails?

Because of the breach of trust between leader and people, the possibilities are endless, and the questions unanswerable. And that is the point. This is no longer merely a scandal about sex. It is about presidential responsibility and trust. It is about a President's use of the individuals around him, and of the faith they put in him as their commander-in-chief. It is about obstruction of justice, and the abuse of a system he was elected to serve.

It is also about the President's vulnerability to political blackmail. How many of those ever involved with Clinton know enough to destroy his administration? And what do they expect for protecting him? Some hypotheticals can be answered. Monica wanted a job and Web Hubbell got four hundred thousand dollars in "fees." But there are many others on the list, known and unknown, the Craig Livingstones and Bruce Lindseys who have explosive material in their possession. What will their pricetags be? Think about the Chinese. According to CIA and FBI reports to the Thompson Committee, China's intelligence apparatus penetrated the White House through the Lincoln bedroom. Is it in the Communists' interest to keep Bill Clinton in power, or to break him? And what is *their* price?

Those who say the presidential crisis is only about sex seem to have forgotten the President's role as the commander-in-chief. If a leader loses the trust of the people who depend on him, how can he continue to lead? Forget the polls, the President is already crippled. During the recent war buildup, he had all the legal authority to send American troops into harm's way, but he did not have the moral authority to appear before his own citizens to rally their support

Overlying all these issues is the matter of justice and social order. At this moment, on this commander's watch, a group of military officers is being court-martialed by the U.S. Army, their careers terminated and their lives ruined for acts hardly different from those the president is alleged to have committed with Paula Jones, Kathleen Willey and Monica Lewinsky.† If there is a difference between the President's case and the accused officers', it is that they are black, and the military has ways of compelling even consenting women to testify against men in the dock, about which the civilian prosecutor can only dream.

And let us not forget Tailhook, which was—after all—only a party at which sex occurred. But because of that party, hundreds of careers were ruined, including those of a Secretary of the Navy and half a dozen admirals who had served their country in time of war. Most of these men were disgraced and stripped of their commands, not because they had personally partaken in sexual frivolities no different from Clinton's, but because they had failed to move swiftly and punitively enough against those who had. Clinton endorsed this verdict and demanded many of these heads himself.

Let one lamb among them stand for all. Commander Robert Stumpf is an eighteen-year veteran of the Naval Air Force, a recipient of the Distinguished Flying Cross, awarded for his bravery in fifty combat missions during the Gulf War. He had come to the Tailhook convention not for sex but to receive an award for commanding the best FA-18 flying squadron during Desert Storm. After the Gulf War, he was made head of the Blue Angels, the Navy's elite flying team. But Commander Stumpf was

† * See "Pilot B," page 82

stripped of this post and his career terminated during Bill Clinton's watch—with the President's full knowledge and acquiescence—not because he attended the Tailhook parties (he did not) but because he was staying in the hotel where they took place.

Let all those who say that this presidential scandal is "only about sex" remember Commander Robert Stumpf and his commander-in-chief. Let them then ask themselves whether it is in the best interests of their country to have double standards for those who lead and those who serve.

Feminist Titanic

As American liberals responded initially to the presidential scandal, one voice remained conspicuously absent from their political chorus. This was the once shrill voice of feminist outrage suddenly, deafeningly, still. For decades we had been assaulted by the mantra "the personal is political." But that was then and this is now. From the chorus on the left the litany we currently hear goes something like this: What President Clinton does in his private life should not be the subject of public concern. Or, as *Politically Incorrect* host Bill Maher put it: "Where's the crime?" Clinton is running the ship of state. Why should we care about his private behavior? As though these latest incidents of sexual misconduct did not take place in the Oval Office, in the seat of government, in the presidential workplace, and as though they did not involve a presidential employee.

What happened to the feminists' concern about disparate power where sexual entanglements take place? Especially when the entanglement involves the nation's chief executive and a starry-eyed, emotionally confused female intern. What place could be more symbolically important to an issue affecting every working woman in America?

Did feminists have a sudden attack of amnesia about their unholy crusade against Clarence Thomas? Here was a man with twenty years of unblemished public service and (unlike Clinton) no history of sexual malfeasance, whom they publicly burned in a shameful witch-hunt. And for what? Certainly not for allegations that he dropped his pants and told a lowly employee of the state to "kiss it." Nor for the alleged seduction of a twenty-one-year-old intern whom he then encouraged to lie to cover up his crime.

Clarence Thomas was subjected to public humiliation and came within an inch of losing a Supreme Court seat for the heinous sins of 1) allegedly mentioning a porn star named Long Dong Silver; 2) allegedly making a joke about a pubic hair on an office Coke can; and 3) allegedly giving vague verbal signals that made a Yale lawyer and experienced civil rights attorney *uncomfortable*. But not so uncomfortable that she didn't stay on the job, ask him for references, and maintain a friendship with him for a decade after. So abominable were these alleged transgressions that righteous feminists and their male amen corner felt no qualms about destroying Thomas's image as a public figure. Indeed, these character assassins of the left, no gracious losers they, continue their ugly crusade and still froth at the mere utterance of Clarence Thomas's name.

In Clinton's case, the evidence of contempt of the feminine gender and abusive patterns of employer behavior is not hopelessly slight or buried in an undiscoverable past. The charges against him are not based on the ten-year old memories of a single individual, but on episodes immediately reported to others. Kathleen Willey was actually observed exiting the Oval Office after an encounter with Clinton, her lipstick smeared and blouse undone. Indeed, with Clinton, we have a plethora of wronged women and their corroborating confidantes. Here, moreover, are not just cases of alleged harassment but also crimes of perjury and cover-up. Here we have a married president sexually involved with an intern less than half his age, alternately discarding her and then using presidential fixers to hush her up and involve her in a felony. Talk about taking advantage.

Of course, the prior trashing of Paula Jones—the precipitant cause of these latest events—roused barely a squeak in feminist circles. The same silence greeted the trashing of Gennifer Flowers years earlier. Discrediting and blaming the victim is a hardly original Clinton strategy. Yet he still gets the feminist vote. By contrast the infamous Senator Specter, despite apologizing for his handling of Hill during Thomas's confirmation, is still ritually hung out to dry by feminist attack squads wherever he appears. Where is the feminist Praetorian guard when Clinton lawyer Robert Bennett and spinmeister James Carville slander Clinton's discarded women as liars, stalkers, and trash?

Who can take self-styled feminists seriously when, in the feminist calculus, only conservatives can be sexual harassers? Liberals like Ted Kennedy and Bill Clinton can have their way with women. Any way they want. They can screw them, abandon them, ruin them—even leave them to drown—and feminists will look the other way. In fact, they will fight to keep the culprits in power.

When these events are over it will be interesting to see whether any of them recognize that their own champion, Hillary Rodham Clinton, is in fact an abuser of her husband's victims, a classic self-hating female, and a self-abused spouse. And with that perception will come how many more lies to protect the guilty, so long as he is a "liberal"?

Bill Clinton

Matt Drudge

Sidney Blumenthal

Drudge Match

In Defense of Matt Drudge

The oddest feature of the affair that pits White House flack Sidney
Blumenthal against Internet gadfly Matt Drudge is probably the most revealing: the failure of the press to defend one of its own. Blumenthal, as everyone knows, has filed a thirty million dollar lawsuit against Drudge for reporting a
rumor that Blumenthal once had a court case for spousal abuse. I should state at the
outset that I am the co-chair of the Matt Drudge Defense Fund (www.cspc.org),
which is raising money to support his legal team. What follows explains why.

Matt Drudge is a self-made entrepreneur, a high-school dropout who made
www.drudgereport.com a national media player—recently ranked number forty in
POV's top one hundred websites—in an arena, where his competitors have names
like Microsoft and *Time*. While the mega-conglomerates deploy battalions of
scribes from glass-towered fortresses scattered across the globe, Drudge operates
alone, from his Hollywood apartment, on a salary of thirty-six thousand dollars a
year. These facts should have made Drudge the underdog favorite in a case that
would seem to pit a White House Goliath against an Internet David.

But they haven't. One obvious reason is that Drudge achieved his status as a
star of the Internet by scooping the big guys. Resentment of the upstart is
undoubtedly a factor working against him. In becoming the first reporter to break
national stories, like the existence of a second Paula Jones (Kathleen Willey) on the
White House staff, Drudge was able to exploit his outsider status to beat the pack.
Another factor is jealousy of the Internet itself. Drudge's apparent recklessness in
reporting a rumor about Blumenthal that turned out to be false evokes the images
of journalistic irresponsibility and informational chaos generated by the freedom
of a medium many already find threatening. The fact that Drudge is an Internet libertarian rather than a statist liberal doesn't help his case either.

Blumenthal is the injured party in the case (although just how injured a sitting
presidential aide can be is another question) and he is currently perceived as the victim of a sloppy gossip columnist of the right. But Blumenthal made his own journalistic bones as a less than scrupulous hit man for the left, notoriously aiming his
punches well below the belt. (Just ask Geraldine Ferraro, whom he portrayed as a
"mafia princess" in a cover story for the *New Republic* at the moment she became the

first woman ever nominated for a vice-presidential spot.). In an attack in the *Washington Post*, ten years ago Blumenthal managed to mangle three crucial details about my own life in the space of three sentences just to discredit me. The fabricated details created the impression that my defection from the left was moral rather than political, and that I had abandoned my Marxist agendas to embrace the ideals not of Hayek but of Hugh Hefner.

Sidney Blumenthal began his career at the socialist tabloid *In These Times*, but his personal ambitions quickly led to stealthier presentations of self, and jobs at the *New Republic* and the *Washington Post*. At the *Post* he managed a brief stint reporting foreign policy on its serious pages until his less than meticulous journalistic methods led to demotion and exile to the Style section (which is where his attack appeared). From thence, his career shifted to the *New Yorker*, where he was made the magazine's White House reporter.

But, here too, political ambition subverted journalistic intention. He had already set his sights on a White House appointment and the sycophancy his pieces began to manifest towards Bill and Hillary soon caused even his editors to wince. When he began lobbying internally against articles being written by other reporters who were critical of the Clintons, and then leaking intelligences to his employers-to-be, *New Yorker* boss Tina Brown yanked him from the beat. Shortly afterwards, Blumenthal joined his wife as a Clinton advisor, the job he had so long been aggressively pursuing. There was a chorus of hoots from betrayed colleagues in the press, and his old employer, the *New Republic*, greeted the announcement of his new position with an item suggesting the Clintons owed him back pay.

This is the man who has taken a holier-than-thou attitude to the offending Matt Drudge for reporting a longstanding "Republican rumor" he was unable to back up. Notified by Blumenthals' lawyers, Drudge immediately apologized for his indiscretion and retracted the item. But Sidney was not to be appeased, and demanded to know the sources. Drudge refused. With Clinton's explicit approval, Sidney slapped Drudge with a thirty million dollar suit. For good measure (and for the deep pockets) his suit also named *America On-Line*, with whom Drudge had a contract.

The effect of this suit is already apparent. A chill wind has swept across the Internet. Blumenthal's attorneys compiled a one hundred and thirty-seven-page summary of the charges, about ten times what lawyers would normally require in such a case. They threw into their indictment chunks of newspaper columns with comments that disparaged Drudge and circulated their document to the entire media. Since lawsuits contain damaging but unsubstantiated charges, lawyers, as a rule, forbid their clients to distribute such filings, even to friends, to avoid the prospect of libel suits in return. But smearing Drudge is one of the objectives of the Blumenthal campaign. In fact, the agenda evident in every move Blumenthal and his patrons have made is to defame and destroy Drudge, as a warning to critics of the Clinton establishment.

Despite all this, Blumenthal has been treated with kid gloves by the nation's press. Though a somewhat sleazy and generally despised member of the journalistic fraternity, Blumenthal, can still flash his Clinton credentials and get results. Joan Konner, head of the Columbia Journalism School and publisher of the *Columbia Journalism Review*, typifies a widespread press attitude. When interviewed for a *Christian Science Monitor* survey on Internet reporters and asked about Drudge, she sneered: "Drudge isn't a reporter, he's your next-door neighbor gossiping over the electronic fence." The reporter, Dirk Smillie, didn't even pause to ask Konner whether she had ever actually read the *Drudge Report*. But when Drudge himself called Konner to account, she confessed that she had never visited his site nor read a single one of the 2,000 stories he had filed. She based her comment on what "others" had written about him.

And there seem to be lots of such others retailing the same party line. Take Karen Breslau, who wrote on the affair for *Newsweek*. When one of her interviewees referred to the damage Blumenthal's friends in the media were inflicting on Drudge's own reputation as an Internet journalist, Breslau snorted "You call Drudge a journalist?"

But the press should put aside snobbish disdain for cyberspace journalism and consider the consequences of abandoning Drudge to the mercies of Blumenthal and his legal juggernaut. Drudge's real offense is to the powerful and the mighty, and the fact that he represents an insurgent medium, which the *ancien régime* is keen to discipline. The cry has gone out: The Internet must be brought under control. Providers like *America On-Line* have been warned: Don't mess around with Internet upstarts. Don't trust individualistic eccentrics who are not under your thumb. Matt Drudge is not only a pretext in this battle for Internet freedom, but a symbol as well.

Confessions of a Right Wing Conspirator

An old writer-friend of mine called the other day to say that he had been advised by a senior editor of the *New Republic* not to have anything to do with my partner Peter Collier and myself because we were "Nazis." The reason? We had organized a fund to defend Matt Drudge, the Internet gadfly who broke the Kathleen Willey and Monica Lewinsky stories and is being sued by White House aide Sidney Blumenthal, the architect of Hillary Clinton's "vast right-wing conspiracy" charges. Every day now, I get calls from the press about my connections to two points on Blumenthal's chart of these right-wing conspirators, Matt Drudge and philanthropist Richard Scaife. And in the *Nation*, the Center for the Study of Popular Culture, the institution that Peter and I created, is itself featured as a point on that chart.

How does it feel to be the focus of a witch-hunt? Actually, it feels very familiar. I grew up in the Cold War Fifties in a family of American Communists. The FBI used to linger on the streets of our neighborhood, charting people's comings and goings. My parents lost their jobs as high school teachers because they would not answer the question had they ever been etc. Once in a junior high school auditorium, when I was thirteen, a group of toughs whom I didn't know put a drape cord around my neck and started shouting, "String him up, he's a Red!"

Unfair as the treatment of my family and our Communist friends was during the McCarthy era, there was a large element of truth in the conspiracy charges. My parents were indeed Communists. They were willing enlistees in a disciplined and secretive movement that did take its orders (and its money) from Moscow and was indeed dedicated to the overthrow of American democracy and the undermining of its security vis-á-vis the Soviet Union. My parents and their friends and most of those who fell into McCarthy's net did accept these loyalties and did subscribe to these goals.

Yet most people agree, and I am one of them, that McCarthy's witch-hunt was a reckless campaign that injured some people who were innocent of any connection to the actual Communist conspiracy and others who while connected to the conspiracy were guiltless of any criminal and/or subversive deeds. McCarthy's true target was not Communists, whom the FBI was already surveilling, but his political opponents in the Democratic Party.

Why then the seeming liberal complacency towards the current White House witch-hunt, whose purpose is to smear and destroy its political critics? As anyone can see, there was no conspiracy in the events leading up to the First Lady's accusation. There is no Communist Party of the right with secret codes and top-down discipline that possesses the ability to give marching orders to anyone. If Monica Lewinsky was planted in the White House, she was planted by Democrats. It was *Newsweek*—no conservative institution—that developed the story that Drudge only made public. Richard Scaife, who is villain #2 in the conspiracy theory, funded investigations that suggested the suicide of Vince Foster might have been a more sinister event. But then Ken Starr, who is villain #1, issued a report refuting the speculations that Scaife had funded while supporting the original suicide claim. What kind of conspiracy is this?

As for my modest role in this matter, I was hardly aware of Drudge's existence

18 · Sex, Lies, & Vast Conspiracies

when I first heard of the Blumenthal suit and offered to introduce Drudge to a lawyer. The lawyer I chose, Manny Klausner, is a well-known civil rights advocate with deep (and very public) ties to the Libertarian Party. The Center for the Study of Popular Culture has long been interested in free speech issues and has defended feminists and Afrocentrists, as well as conservatives, on First Amendment issues. Its legal arm spearheaded the battle against speech codes on college campuses. We attained some notoriety when we forced a vice-chancellor at the University of California to undergo "sensitivity training" in the First Amendment after he banned a fraternity for producing a T-shirt the PC crowd didn't like. (We were even criticized by George Will in one of his *Newsweek* columns because he didn't get the joke.) So we were in the field of free speech well before the punitive White House suit against Matt Drudge.

We do get funds from the Scaife foundations in addition to twenty other foundations and fifteen thousand individuals. Why is Richard Scaife, whom I have met and talked to twice in my life, being demonized as though he were the mastermind of a plot to get the President? Why is the Center for the Study of Popular Culture, which has sought only to defend a journalist from what it perceived as a punitive and chilling attack, dragged into the plot?

The answer is obvious from previous witch-hunts. It is to deflect attention from the real issues; it is to conjure fantasy demons in order to smear and then cripple real opponents. The question to be asked is why, given the black record of witch-hunts of the past, the country is so tolerant of this latest attack?

Character Assassination as a Political Weapon

The editor of the *New Republic* referred to in the previous chapter, who called Peter Collier and me Nazis because of our defense of Matt Drudge was an old friend named John Judis. Here is how it happened: After writing a defense of Drudge, that appeared in *Salon* magazine, I received a call from Peter, my writing partner and *Heterodoxy* co-editor. He himself had just been called by our mutual friend, Ron Radosh, whose article on his old Communist summer camp appeared in *Heterodoxy*. Radosh had contacted Judis to suggest he read the article, but John replied he wouldn't read anything printed in *Heterodoxy*, saying that we were "Nazis" (a charge he later withdrew). The occasion of his wrath was the fact that I had set up a defense fund for Matt Drudge. Peter promptly e-mailed Judis the following message:

John:
Drudge, *Heterodoxy*, Susan Estrich, Kinsley, Nazis. Yikes.
Collier

Peter's reference was to the fact that Susan Estrich and Michael Kinsley had also defended Drudge. His e-mail drew a reply from Judis:

I assume your letter was prompted by a conversation I had with Ron Radosh this afternoon, since I haven't talked to you in ages. You need to know a little background. Ron brought up *Heterodoxy*. I said, as I have said before to him, that I was pissed off about Horowitz's defense of that scumbag Drudge. Radosh attributed my position to my being friends with Sid Blumenthal, and instead of blowing up at him as I should have (the implication is that the only reason I defended him on the George Washington thing was because he was a friend of mine†), I started railing about Nazis. I don't think Horowitz is a Nazi, but I do think that his position is detestable. I wrote him a letter at the time but it was returned because he no longer lives at the address to which I sent it. Assuming you are in cahoots on this stuff, I'll send it to you and you can forward it to him if you desire.
John

What follows is the letter to me, that was never sent, which Judis e-mailed to Peter:

11/19/97
Dear David:
This morning, a mutual friend of ours urged me to read your articles on Sid Blumenthal and the *Drudge Report*. Rather than responding simply to him (I think I said something to the effect that I'd rather eat dogshit), I thought I would tell you what I thought of your leading the defense of Mr. Drudge.
Let me make the point indirectly through two anecdotes:
1) When the *Drudge Report* first came out, one of my friends called me that afternoon to ask whether I'd seen it and what I knew of Sid's private life. This person, who didn't know Sid, assumed the report was true.

---

†The incident referred to was an attempt by leftist academics led by Eric Foner to keep Radosh from a faculty position at George Washington University. Judis generously provided testimony in Radosh's behalf. Radosh was eventually allowed to teach at the school.

I read it myself, and reading about court records, wondered, too, whether Sid hadn't concealed a part of himself from me all these years. Afterwards, I talked to several people who knew Sid and Jackie socially better than I did who thought the report was preposterous, but until the hoax was fully revealed, I still had lingering doubts. The point is this: there is no slander so insidious or so subversive to a person's reputation and character as a charge of wife-beating, especially when backed up with claims about court records. It can lead a friend of twenty years to harbor doubts about them. That's why law schools use this kind of charge as a model for slander and defamation.

2) After the hoax was revealed, I suggested to one of the editors at the *New Republic* that they run a short about it, noting, among other things, the connection to AOL, but this editor, knowing Mike Kelly's animosity toward Sid (at least the equal in ferocity of your own) hesitated to suggest it. To my surprise, Kelly brought it up himself and insisted on running a short. His one concern was that even mentioning such a charge in the course of explaining it was a hoax could lend credence to it. In this case, Kelly was willing to put aside his feelings toward Sid because it was a question of principle—of someone attacking someone's reputation in the most scurrilous manner and using the new power of the Internet to do so. Kelly also believed, as I do, that it was important to sue in this instance, because it is important to establish a precedent so that other would-be journalists are deterred from following the example of Mr. Drudge and so that publishers, such as America On-Line, are deterred from promoting these kind of scumbags.

I'd draw a very sharp contrast between your conduct and Kelly's. The mark of a moral person is the ability, upon occasion, to transcend one's own resentments and hatreds, as well as one's loves and enthusiasms. Kelly was able to do it. You are not. The main difference between your defense of Drudge in the '90s and your defense of Huey Newton or *Los Siete* †† during the '60s is that in the latter cases, you still had a smidgen of principle. I detest what you are doing.

> Yours,
>
> John

---

†† *Los Siete de La Raza* (The Seven of the Race). A group of Chicanos accused of murdering a policeman, they were a cause celebre of the Sixties left and *Ramparts*, the magazine that Peter Collier and I edited. *Los Siete* were acquitted and subsequently several of their members were re-arrested and convicted of other crimes, including murder.

Peter replied to this e-mail from John:

2/14/98

John:
I put the letter of 11/19 in the trash receptacle of my e-mail program. If you want to send it to David, go ahead. He will send you one, I'm sure, by return mail that will be equally morally uppity and probably even more (and I have to say, more justly) contemptuous.

He will accuse you of ignoring how the item was published and retracted. He will point out that there is an illuminating sequel in the events that monopolize the news today. He will note that Blumenthal is a loathsome individual figure who is doubtless, at this very moment, blackguarding someone, somewhere, somehow, since that is his only discernable talent.

If I know David, he will take you to task particularly for the last paragraph of this still-unsent letter of yours, which won't be difficult, since you've given him a target as big as a barn with what could easily be interpreted as a morally imbecilic proposition about supporting criminal gangs in the '60s being some sort of misguided principle that can still be said to travel well, in extreme rhetorical instances such as the case at hand, in the '90s.

"Innocently" supporting murderers in the '60s: morally ok. Less innocently supporting an Internet gossip monger in the '90s: morally criminal. This is a weird moral calculus, my friend.

And after all these bitternesses are exhumed, then where will we all be? Nowhere. Worse than nowhere. Which is why I didn't forward your letter to David.

Some things are better off left unsaid.
      Cheers,
      Peter

Peter and I then had a conversation, and I asked him to retrieve John's e-mail from his trash, and send it to me. I then replied to John myself:

2/14/98

Dear John,
I have Peter's trash of your e-mail of November in which you explain why you have washed your hands of me, and "detest" what I do, apparently

because I have come to the defense of Matt Drudge. This makes me a con-
spirator, apparently, in the plot to wound Sidney Blumenthal through unkind
and inaccurate words that misrepresent the person you presume him to be.
Peter has also sent me the reply he wrote in my behalf, and while I concur in
his observations, they seem nonetheless incomplete. For me the attack in
your letter also broaches basic issues about the nature of our political dis-
course and I am, therefore, answering you in my own voice.

Over the last ten years I have kept in touch with you, partly for old
times' sake, and partly because I thought you were a man of integrity and
would keep faith with the past we shared. Though we no longer shared agendas, I thought there might even come a time when you would provide testimony against the powerful attacks and distortions of my life and Peter's that
have been direct consequences of our political defection.

As you can see this touches directly on the issues you raise about the
misrepresentation of your friend at the hands of Matt Drudge. For Peter and
I have been the target of far more relentless distortion and more calculated
slander than your friend Sid. In terms of actual wounds inflicted by mean-
spirited and vicious misrepresentations of self, as of damages incurred,
Blumenthal does not begin to know what pain is. Or, evidently, how to deal
with it.

In view of your attack on me now, it is something of an irony that I
thought you might be up to the task of one day defending me against political slanders. I was perhaps misled by the fact that you were willing to enter-
tain any overtures at all from me, when almost everyone Peter and I had
known and befriended in the community of the left had turned on us with an
irrational hatred when our politics changed. The passion of these newly mint-
ed enemies was so intense that we could no longer count on those who had
witnessed what we had done to respect the integrity of a single fact about our
lives, once that fact was put into question. Were Peter and David holy rollers
of the ideological sects, partisans of mindless extremes? Were they the real
authors of the crimes they accused other of committing? It was left to us, and
to others who had second thoughts, to remember that we were not.

Consider how total this attack on our reality has been. While an almost
universal hatred has been directed at Peter and me by our former comrades,
we are the ones accused by them of malice; of having acted out extremist
fantasies in the past and of being driven only by our hatred of old friends in
the present.

But your personal tolerance of me was not the only factor that encouraged my misplaced trust. I was also impressed that in your own writing you made a significant effort to be fair to intellectual opponents on the right, like Bill Buckley, whose biographer you became. You made a modest specialty of conservative intellectuals and even of "renegades" from the left like James Burnham and Whittaker Chambers. I respected this, and it encouraged me to hope that this spirit of fairness might one day prompt you to examine our careers and counteract the politically motivated efforts to defame us as a way of dismissing anything we had to say. Only this month, for example, your friend Paul Berman described me as a "demented lunatic" in the foremost intellectual journal of the left, as someone who was a Leninist fanatic both before his second thoughts and afterwards—lies on both counts.

From the time Peter and I announced our political change of heart in a piece in the *Washington Post* some thirteen years ago, and then organized a conference of other "second thoughters," we were greeted by a wall of hate erected by our former comrades. Your friend Sidney played a significant part in creating that wall. In a signature piece on our conference that appeared in the *Washington Post*, he caricatured us as political buffoons and right-wing extremists. It was the beginning of a campaign to degrade our humanity and marginalize us in the culture. In the same article, Sidney portrayed me as a callow narcissist who had abandoned his principles and his children to flee to the flesh-pots of Beverly Hills. Every word he wrote was false, but there was no way for me to respond or to clear my name.

And that was just the beginning. Over the last ten years, the attacks on Peter and myself have continued. We have been portrayed as murderers (by your friends Hertzberg and Berman), as political criminals, as racists and homophobes, and always as shrill and monomaniacal ideologues to whom no self-respecting intellectual should pay the slightest serious attention. This is the culture war, John, and it has been successfully waged against us in the very precincts that you roam. Peter and I have written the only books by veterans of the Sixties left that challenge its myths. They are primary sources for the period as well as analytical texts about its meanings. But in college curricula across the country you will rarely find references to *Destructive Generation* or *Second Thoughts* (or now *Radical Son*). The tenured left has seen to that. Instead you will find texts by Sixties loyalists Angela Davis, Todd Gitlin, and even Huey Newton. Racist anti-semites like Stokely Carmichael will visit these same campuses as well-paid guests, and radical ideologues will be invited to serve as commencement speakers. We get no such invitations. The campaign of political libel conducted by Sidney and

and your friends, though it has not silenced us as they intended, has not been without its successes either.

Now I will tell you something that you may not believe, but that is true nonetheless. I don't harbor any personal malice for Sidney Blumenthal, nor is any such animus the reason I came to the defense of Matt Drudge. Any discomfort that Sidney inflicted through his caricature in the *Post* was washed away when I was able to write my own story in *Radical Son* and thus correct his misrepresentations about my family and my motives. Moreover, the malice towards Peter and me and the general misrepresentation of our politics is so generic to the left that it would be foolish to load responsibility on one man. If Matt Drudge had deliberately libeled Sidney for political ends and revealed a malicious intent to destroy him in the process, I assure you I would not have come to Drudge's aid.

Nor would I hesitate to have done what Michael Kelly did in printing a correction of the Drudge error. The fact is, as Peter has pointed out, that Drudge did this himself and did so immediately on being informed of his mistake. And his retraction was reported throughout the press and to a far greater audience than the original error.

What then is the purpose of Sidney's thirty million dollar lawsuit? Surely not to send a warning to other writers as you suggest. The suit and the retraction already perform that function. My own piece in *Salon* about the affair was censored in several of its parts simply because the editors were afraid of a similar suit. I reported, for example, that Sidney had been shifted to the Style section of the *Post* when his editors became unhappy about his less than scrupulous journalistic methods. This was factually true, but still too risky for *Salon*'s editors in the litigious climate Sidney and his lawyers have created. Is this an atmosphere that you, as a writer, want to encourage?

You make a claim of special heinousness for Drudge's offense. You write that there is no slander so insidious or subversive of character as the charge of wife-beating. Really? More insidious than Berman's charge that Peter and I were complicit in the murder of our friend, and then sought to shift the blame to others?

Let's take your claim about wife-beating charges at face value. Have you considered the case of Don Sipple, the Republican pollster accused of wife-beating by your friends at *Mother Jones*? Perhaps you'll remember that this was the immediate provocation of Drudge's own sin. *Mother Jones* also accused Sipple on the basis of "court records" and did not, like Drudge, qualify the charge as "rumor." Drudge reported the rumor about Blumenthal as one that Republicans were going to surface in order to revenge and neutralize the attack on Sipple. Unlike Blumenthal, who suffered no material damages, Sipple actually lost his job, and had no friends at *Newsweek*, the *New York Times*, *Time*, or the *Washington Post* to report and support his side of the story.

Do you have any idea of what the basis for the charge against Sipple was? The impression given in the media was that he had been convicted in a court of law of beating his wife. When I looked at the original article in *Mother Jones*, it was somewhat of a shock to discover that the charge was actually an unproven claim made by a scorned ex-wife in the course of a bitter custody battle. I have no idea of the truth of this charge, but neither does *Mother Jones* or you. Yet a man has been seriously damaged as a result. Where is your outrage over the insidious subversion of Don Sipple's life?

Here is what is so perverse in your anguish over Sid. Unlike Sipple (or Peter and myself), Blumenthal commands enormous influence and power as a presidential aide with a large network of friends in the press. He was able to reach millions with his side of the story immediately. In context, such pain as he incurred, though I am sure it was serious, was minimized. By contrast, ten years ago, when I went to Richard Harwood, the ombudsman of the *Washington Post*, to point out the lies that Sidney had written about me, Harwood shrugged his shoulders sympathetically, and suggested I write a letter to the editor, which few would notice. He did remove the offending column from the *Post*'s weekly national edition, a small but gratefully acknowledged gesture. On the other hand, your Sid, now cognizant of the facts and wholly unrepentant, made sure that the slander would reach a wider audience by reprinting the lies he had written, uncorrected, in a book of his collected articles called *Pledging Allegiance*.

Certainly no one in politics is immunized from name-calling, gross misrepresentation and unfounded accusation. That is deplorable but it is also the territory, and has been from time immemorial. In such an environment, all anyone can ask is to be able to respond to the slanders that are made and attempt to correct them. Occupying a high political ground, Blumenthal had powers of correction that most of us lack. He should be the last to whine, let alone sue. That you and Blumenthal seem so refreshingly thin-skinned only reveals how protected you are, as members of the left, by a liberal media sympathetic to you, and by the relative civility of the conservative press.

In the end, Blumenthal's suit has only one set of agendas: to destroy Drudge, to run him out of the business, to discredit him, and shut him up along with all the other Clinton adversaries from Gennifer Flowers to Paula Jones. In these battles the White House is a Goliath from which you would normally keep your distance. So, why your hostility to the Internet David? The error Drudge made in passing on the rumor about your friend hardly reflects a pattern in his journalism. He is so innocent of such smears and of the suits that can attend them that he didn't even have an attorney until I put him in touch with one.

The same cannot be said for your friend. Sidney no doubt has the best legal advice money and his proximity to the Clintons can secure. His lawyers showed no qualms about circulating his one hundred and thirty-seven-page suit, filled with unsubstantiated charges against Drudge to the entire media (a practice that invites a libel claim in return). Moreover, he is supported by an armada of prominent left-wing journalists for whom liberal distortion and personal abuse are the *lingua franca* of their craft—Joe Conason, Christopher Hitchens, Frank Rich, Eric Alterman, Alex Cockburn, and Robert Scheer.

It is Sid, isn't it, whose new career is that of the Clintons' shadow McCarthy, architect of the "vast right-wing conspiracy" charge that Hillary dropped on TV the other morning and that has reporters calling me daily. In the reigning paranoia that Sidney has stoked in his job as Clinton attack dog, I have become part of his infamous conspiracy chart because I set up a fund to pay Drudge's legal bills. This ugly claim is what Maureen Dowd identifies as the Clinton "doomsday strategy" and what Stephanopoulos recently described as the determination "to take everybody down with him"—interns, witnesses, journalists—by exposing their dirty secrets to the public. I'm sure the nine hundred and forty-one FBI files the Clintons illegally appropriated will come in handy for such purposes.

It was only a year ago that Peter and I hosted an event in Los Angeles you attended as our guest. The meeting was warm with nostalgia, and for our part we made every effort to put you at ease in the environment you were entering. Yet, cordial as our relations seemed to be, you didn't call me about this matter or even bother to make sure that your letter was put in my hands. You chose instead to attack me behind my back, and to warn our mutual friend Ron Radosh of the contagion involved in any contact with us, that *Heterodoxy* was now off limits if he wanted respectability. "Don't write for *Heterodoxy*. I won't read it. I'd rather eat dogshit," is what you apparently said.

And, so, you have developed your own way of dehumanizing Peter and me, and of becoming part of the *kulturkampf* against us. This must be why you have abandoned your usual judgment in embracing a scoundrel like Blumenthal (or at least his scoundrel acts). And this is why, while championing Sid, you have never thought to correct the insidious slanders directed at us in the magazines you write for and among the audiences you reach. An assessment of our work that recognized its seriousness and that corrected the caricatures of our character and allegiances would have been a natural sequel to your pieces on previously despised defectors like Burnham and Chambers. The difference is that they are safely dead and we are not. For the people you call your friends and whose praise and plaudits you seek, Peter and I are radioactive—political untouchables, as we have been for the nearly fifteen years since those first lies from Blumenthal's pen. Now, what lawsuit is going to give us redress from that?

David

David Brock

Clarence Thomas

Michael Lind

David Horowitz

Conspiracies

The Liberal Media and the Affair of David Brock

In the April 1998 issue of *Esquire*, David Brock, the slayer of Anita Hill, the outer of Paula Jones, the relentless scourge of sanctimonious liberals goes down on his knees to plant an unseemly kiss on the presidential posterior. In an Open Letter, Brock apologizes to Clinton for not "really" being interested in "good government" when he wrote his *American Spectator* story on the governor's sexcapades in Arkansas and use of state troopers to pimp his scores. The *Spectator* exposé, which Brock modestly claims to be the true origin of the present presidential crisis, was motivated by more primitive ambitions than ordinary journalism: "I wanted to pop you right between the eyes."

This confession is but the latest bizarre chapter in David Brock's unpleasant political odyssey. The first version of his tale appeared nine months earlier in the July *Esquire* under the headline "I Was A Right-Wing Hit Man." Promoting the article was a staged photo of Brock tied to a tree, one nipple seductively exposed. The editors didn't say whether he was waiting to be shot, or to nurse.

"Writer Tells Truth, Conservatives Can't Handle It" is the way Brock would like to spin the story of his exit from the political right. His opening salvo was hailed by hit men of the left like *Slate*'s Jacob Weisberg, who followed the *mea culpa* with a premature obituary for conservatives titled "The Conintern: Republican Thought Police." Here, a theme only suggested by Brock—that conservatives have become the very enemy they despise—is presented as a foregone conclusion by the enemy himself.

As in all such capers, however, there is the story and the story.

David Brock first made a name for himself as the only reporter who bothered to track down the details of Anita Hill's life and career. While the rest of the journalistic community lazily accepted her own version of who she was, Brock took the trouble to look for himself. In *The Real Anita Hill* he gathered enough evidence to blow a barn-size hole through the principal claims that had made Hill's case against Clarence Thomas seem credible—that she had no ulterior agenda in pressing her charges; that she was a put-upon, apolitical, and even conservative, victim; that she was too shy, too timid, or too unsophisticated to have pressed sexual harassment charges at the time the incidents allegedly took place, ten years in the past.

Through painstaking legwork, Brock showed the accuser's reality to be quite different from her story. She was, in fact, an ambitious and aggressive climber, fashionably steeped in left-wing feminism, with a penchant for lying when faced with adversity. Asked to leave her first Washington legal job for reasons of incompetence, she found refuge in the leftist victimology she had picked up at Yale, which provided a convenient cover for personal inadequacy. Ironically, it was by claiming she had been sexually harassed at Wald, Harkrader, and Ross that she originally won the sympathy of Clarence Thomas, who generously provided her with a new job in his office. Through diligent reporting of Hill's career before, during, and after the Thomas hearings, Brock convincingly established a character pattern of petty ambition and spiteful revenge that served to explain Hill's otherwise inexplicable behavior before, during, and after her celebrated performance in front of the nation.

For this valuable effort, Brock was pilloried mercilessly in the liberal press—still the press of record and respect. In a typically overheated attack, *New York Times* columnist Anthony Lewis characterized the book as "sleaze with footnotes," only to confess privately afterwards that he had "breezed hastily" through it before publishing his condemnation. His performance was typical. Brock was contemptuously dismissed as "not only a sleazebag but the occasion in others for sleazebaggery," by writers like Garry Wills, who went along with the same wolf-pack that had picked over Thomas's garbage, video-rental lists, and divorce papers and then rushed to the support of an embittered former employee peddling slander based on a ten-year-old incident that no one outside herself could corroborate. In another gutter attack, the *New York Times* poison pen Frank Rich accused Brock of hating the entire female sex—not so subtly outing him as a homosexual in the process. Rich calculated that this would damage Brock's standing in the right, having convinced himself that his previous attacks on conservatives as sub-human, homophobic bigots was something more than vacuous libel.

In the event, Brock's outing had no adverse effect on his reputation in conservative circles. On the contrary, his star kept rising as a hero who had single-handedly accomplished what a self-respecting, non-partisan press should have done in the first place—check out the story of a character-assassin and spare the nation the disgraceful spectacle of Hill's malicious public assault. When Brock followed his coup by interviewing the Arkansas troopers moonlighting as panderers for the governor in Little Rock, his stock among conservatives soared even higher.

At this juncture, New York's only conservative publisher, The Free Press, offered Brock a one million dollar advance to do an investigation of—what else?—the career of Hillary Clinton. Given what already was known about Hillary's luck in commodity markets, ambitious derailment of her husband's first term, domic-

tions of justice blatant enough to make Nixon's look amateur, and rumored liaison with Vince Foster, expectations about a Brock investigation were predictably high. A first printing of two hundred thousand copies was announced, enough to make the book a runaway best-seller. *Newsweek* arranged to run an excerpt, and a major book tour was planned.

But somewhere along the way Brock had lost his journalistic bearings. When the book was finally delivered, none of the expected goods came with it. The response at *Newsweek* was typical: "The editors are in tears that you don't have Hillary in bed with Vince, or at least someone," was the message The Free Press relayed to him, along with the news that *Newsweek* would pass on the excerpt. Not only did Brock not have anything new to reveal, his account of the old was something less than incisive. So disappointing was his version of Hillary's Whitewater dealings, in fact, that James B. Stewart chided him in the *New York Times* for unnecessarily bending over backwards to defend the First Lady on points which were, after all, indefensible.

As the rest of the media became aware that the reporter had failed to deliver a story, network appearances and scheduled interviews were cancelled, while others didn't materialize. The national author tour was aborted before it even got started, and the stacks of books from the two hundred thousand first printing piled high in Barnes & Noble and other chains, were pasted with "50% Off" stickers. *The Seduction of Hillary Rodham* had been remaindered almost before it was even published, and the publisher was looking at a total loss.

Brock had violated the most elementary principle of best-seller marketing: Don't defeat the expectations you raise. Fans of Brock, who expected an expose, felt let down by his kid glove treatment of a woman they despised. Fans of Hillary, who hated Brock for exposing Anita Hill, couldn't care less that he was now willing to bend over backwards to give another feminist icon a break. Neither audience bought the book. No surprise here.

But David Brock *was* surprised. And his reaction to failure, just like Anita Hill's, was to go into denial and come out attacking. Brock concluded that conservatives were out to punish him because he had "told the truth." He was disinvited to parties. He was no longer a hero. Conservatives, as he put it, could not forgive him for being "somewhat sympathetic" to Hillary. This version of events is written all over the anecdote with which Brock opens his kiss-off to conservatives in *Esquire*. The anecdote tells how Brock was disinvited to an A-list party of Washington conservatives and congressional staffers. "Given what's happened," Brock quotes a voice-mail message the hostess left him, "I don't think you'd be comfortable at the party." The impression left is that because Brock was soft on

Hillary he was no longer welcome among conservatives who had once been his best friends.

This is what is generously called a half-truth. What Brock withholds from the reader is that the anger directed at him came from congressional staffers who had helped him with his manuscript on the understanding that he would not reveal his sources. Brock had reneged on the agreement and blown their cover. In other words, it was the betrayal of confidences and friends rather than party lines that was at the heart of the matter.

David Brock is apparently incapable of confronting shortcomings for which he has only himself to blame. Egged on by promptings of the grandiose self, he has transformed his personal screw-ups into an epic case. "The age of reporting is dead," he writes as though his was the story of a William Randolph Hearst or a Rupert Murdoch who could resonate with the *zeitgeist* itself. And then: "My side turned out to be as dirty as theirs." And again: "There is no 'liberal movement' to which [liberal] journalists are attached and by which they can be blackballed in the sense that there is a self-identified, hardwired conservative movement' that can function as a kind of neo-Stalinist thought police that rivals anything I knew at Berkeley." In short, that can punish David Brock.

This from a man whose conservative publisher accepted his final manuscript ("With my publishers blessing, I was faithful to my reporting," Brock reports without noticing the implication) and put out two hundred thousand copies of a book which didn't sell, adding hundreds of thousands to the already million-dollar loss. And this, from a man who (at the time his *Esquire* article was published) was *still* the journalistic star of the Right's biggest and most Clinton-antagonistic magazine, with a half-million-dollar contract to prove it. In fact, Brock wrote his *Esquire* kiss-off to the right on the *American Spectator*'s dime! Its managing editor, Wlady Plesczynski, had passionately defended Brock's book to this very writer six months before Brock's article, and had done so at a "Dark Ages Weekend," the big conservative New Year's bash to which the supposedly ostracized Brock was an invited panelist. In his talk he deplored the "scandal-mongering" of some conservative critics of Clinton, as the crotchety author of a big flop, Brock was no longer quite the star he had once been, and his reception was probably less deferential than his *amour propre* deemed appropriate. On the other hand, the *Weekly Standard* published his talk. Some censorship!

David Brock's problem is not conservatism, it is narcissism. And once he published his *mea culpa*, it became politics as well. In the *Esquire* article, Brock declared his independence from the right, even as he re-affirmed his conservative views. Apparently, he thought he could be a free-floating journalist sans partisan baggage, accepted as a writer for the liberal media the way he was still accepted at the *American Spectator*.† But the fall-out from his article was already radioactive.

Salon weighed in with a piece by David Futurelle ("Who's Sorry Now?") that reflected the favored liberal response: *You were a sleazebag then, and you're a sleazebag now.* But *Slate* went a step further, deciding to seize the opportunity for a conservative blood-letting and let the score-settling wait for later. Jacob Weisberg's lead article in *Slate* was an attempt to deliver the death-blow to any further intellectual pretensions by conservatives. Weisberg is the man who once filed a cover piece for *New York Magazine* featuring head-shots of six prominent conservatives under a screaming three-inch headline labeling them "UN-AMERICANS."

In his *Slate* article, Weisberg predictably upped Brock's ante: "The party where humorless thought police work to enforce a rigid ideological discipline isn't made up of Democrats. It comprises Republicans . . . . Brock portrays a political subculture in which loyalty to the cause means everything, truth very little." As a liberal journalist, Weisberg is confident, of course, that he is under no obligation to check Brock's claims with a single reportorial call to sources. Who, in the universe of like-minded scribes, would call him to account?

Not content with a passing hit, Weisberg actually defines the relation between Left and Right as that between free men and slaves: "The treatment of Brock has no parallel among liberals. A few left-wing journalists, such as Nat Hentoff and Christopher Hitchens, have caught flak for dissenting from the conventional liberal position on abortion. But . . . ."

This distortion of the political realities of the literary culture is one that I take almost personally. Peter Collier and I were best-selling authors, once editors of the largest magazine of the Left, and sought-after writers by liberal magazines—until we strayed from the party line that Weisberg pretends doesn't exist. In my own case, it took more than ten years before an invitation came to write for a non-conservative magazine again (*Salon*). Our mutual friend, Ronald Radosh was literally banned from writing on the subject of Nicaragua while still a masthead editor of *Dissent*. The ban was triggered by his political incorrectness and imposed by the magazine's founder and icon of democratic socialism, Irving Howe.

But this is far from a personal story. If liberal journalists lack a party line, perhaps Weisberg can refer us to the brave liberal souls who did not go along with the wolf-pack that descended on Bork and Thomas, or who may have suggested in some venue I overlooked that the Clinton obstructions of justice and the White

---

† Six months after this article was written, Brock's contract with the *Spectator* was cancelled because Brock had not performed according to its terms. The issue was not the content of articles produced, but the lack of articles as called for in the contract. He had written only three in an entire year, for which he was paid seventy thousand dollars.

House abuse of governmental agencies match (let alone overshadow) Watergate in their implications for constitutional order. Perhaps he will let us all know the names of those who departed from the politically correct line on AIDS. Perhaps he will give us the honor roll of those who broke ranks to describe the feminist witch-hunt of America's military. Or perhaps Weisberg can refer us to a liberal journalist who exercised his profession's legendary skepticism in writing about the recent release of the convicted murderer and former Black Panther, Geronimo Pratt.†

As for the conservative lock-step, what a hoot. In the six months prior to Weisberg's *Slate* article, Arianna Huffington has attacked every conservative leader Weisberg could name, without noticeably diminishing her invitations to parties or service on the boards of conservative think tanks. Bill Kristol is regularly slammed by Republican leaders, and Pat Buchanan was labeled a "fascist" by both the *American Spectator* and Bill Bennett without diminishing his presence at conservative conferences. Newt Gingrich has been viciously caricatured on the covers of *National Review* and the *Weekly Standard*, which announced his "meltdown" and ran an article pillorying him as "Political Road Kill." Howard Kurtz, in a survey of *l'affaire* Brock for the *Washington Post*, managed to get three major conservative journalists—Robert Novak, William Safire, and Bill Kristol—to complain on the record, in the liberal press, about other conservatives, conceding that "The idea that conservative journalists have always marched in lock-step with with their ideological brethren is something of a myth." So much for the "Conintern."

As a former partisan of the Left, I can testify to how exhilarating it is to breathe free in the conservative intellectual air. Conservatism is a tent so big that the conventional wisdom is to doubt its coherence as a political movement. The impending break-up of the right in the post-Communist world because there will be nothing now to hold the squalling wings of conservatism together is almost a journalistic cliche. Today, in the pages of magazines that Weisberg describes as under party discipline, conservatives war over immigration, abortion, drug policy, homosexuality, openings to China, the place of religion, the credibility of supply-side economics, and the sanity of Jude Wanniski and Jack Kemp.

By contrast, liberals war over how to position themselves to get elected. How many serious clashes of values are there in the liberal ranks? Are there liberals who view the ending of welfare as a positive good, who would like to see the non-defense budget drastically cut, who want to reduce the capital gains tax to zero? Consider a more volatile issue like affirmative action. Anyone who inquires, quickly learns that there are many, many deeply troubled liberal consciences who oppose racial preferences but are afraid to express themselves publicly. Is there a single prominent lib-

---

† See "Geronimo Pratt," page 106

eral who has dared to remain publicly faithful to the civil rights principles enunciated by Martin Luther King, or who has had the courage to denounce racial discrimination in the Nineties in the same moral voice that liberals used to denounce racial discrimination in the Sixties? If so, I certainly missed it.

Or consider the parallel case to Brock's original book. Two liberal reporters, Jane Mayer and Jill Abramson, followed *The Real Anita Hill* with a counter-volume about Clarence Thomas called *Strange Justice* (even the pun signals who the sleaze artists are). This turned out to be an unoriginal but unerringly sordid personal attack on the only Supreme Court justice who is also an African American, a man who rose against extreme odds of poverty and racial oppression to achieve high office, and who has only a single blemish on his entire public career (and how many public figures can say that?). That "blemish," of course, is the result of an unproven libel about alleged events in a distant past, coming from an embittered, unreliable, and partisan source whose gripings never should have been provided a public platform in the first place.

Strange Justice was promoted and celebrated by the same shameless chorus that prevented Brock's own investigation from being taken seriously outside the conservative ghetto. Was there a single liberal journalist or reviewer who broke ranks to condemn the atrocity the left committed on the public figure of Clarence Thomas and deplore the character assassination of an extraordinary African-American jurist?

Or consider the other side of Weisberg's equation: In the wake of the partisan lynching of Justice Thomas, Senator Orrin Hatch accepted, without demurral, Clinton's nomination of Ruth Bader Ginsburg, a long-time ideological leader of the feminist left. Was Hatch read out of the conservative movement for this political surrender? Did any conservative journalist rummage through Ginsburg's garbage and personal secrets in order to smear and taint her, as liberals did Thomas and Bork? Was there a relentless Republican interrogation at the hearings aimed at ferreting out her ideological commitments? Did conservatives join in any effort to destroy her ability to be a role model to women, in the way liberals closed ranks to destroy Thomas' public persona and keep him from becoming an inspiration to his community?

The media is so utterly and pervasively dominated by the liberal culture that liberals have lost the ability to see who they are and what they do. Or to really give a damn. We are all driven by the sense of our own righteousness, but normally others are around to keep our hubris in check. When ours is the only voice audible, that becomes the only truth we hear.

Predictably, David Brock has now dropped his ambivalence and his bid for independent status, and moved on to the greener pastures of the conservative-bashing press. In his April "open letter," he claims that he has seen the light. "If sexual witch-hunts become the way to win in politics, if they become our politics altogether, we can and will destroy everyone in public life." An interesting concept that manages to smear—witch-hunt style—a whole class of people without offering any evidence to support it. Brock's new mentor? Why, it's Sidney Blumenthal, the genie behind the First Lady's "vast right-wing conspiracy" hysteria.

Michael Lind and the Right Wing Cabal

Two winters ago, while working on my autobiography *Radical Son*, I received a phone call from my friend Ronald Radosh telling me about an article Michael Lind had written for the socialist magazine *Dissent*. The article was called "The Death of Intellectual Conservatism" and was Lind's explanation of the political transformation that had led him to abandon his career as a political journalist on the right and join the anti-conservative crowd on the left. Lind's conversion was announced with great fanfare and accepted by all and sundry as a "God That Failed" in reverse.

One thing that struck me about this was that prior to the appearance of Lind's article, and despite the fact that we were both members of a relatively small community of conservative intellectuals, I had only been vaguely conscious of his existence. Although I was an inveterate reader of conservative magazines and books, and familiar with most if not all of the intellectual lights of this movement, I knew Lind only as a name on the masthead of Irving Kristol's foreign policy magazine, the *National Interest*, and as the author of one or two articles whose subjects and arguments had not left a lasting impression.

Despite Lind's obscurity, there were reasons for the interest which the news of his apostasy aroused in me. To begin with, there was the appearance of a parallel career, as someone who seemed to be stepping onto a path that both Radosh and I had previously trod, albeit in the opposite direction. The path had begun in 1952 when Radosh and I had gotten to know each other at a meeting of his chapter of the Labor Youth League—a Communist Party front in lower Manhattan—where I had come to recruit writers for the *Daily Worker's* "youth page." The "page" lasted for only one issue, but Ron and I became lifelong friends, and in 1987, Radosh was one of the former radicals Peter Collier and I recruited for a "Second Thoughts Conference" we held at the Grand Hyatt in Washington, D.C. We had assembled a group of former Sixties radicals who were fed up with the anti-American passions and totalitarian romances of the left and ready to say goodbye to all that. The intellectuals grouped around *Dissent* whom Michael Lind now counts as his new comrades, were among the most vocal in attacking our second thoughts about the Sixties as "renegade" and over-wrought.

The second reason for my interest in Lind's political conversion was a long-running dialogue between Radosh and myself about whether we should have wound up as conservatives at all. Radosh was, in fact, still on the editorial board of *Dissent*, though more in name than anything else at the time of Lind's conversion. He had been banned from writing in its pages by *Dissent's* editor and guiding spirit Irving Howe because of his opposition to the Sandinista dictatorship. Having forbade Radosh from writing on the subject of Nicaragua to the *Dissent* audience, Howe then pressured him, through emissaries, to resign from its board. He stopped short of actually removing Radosh only because another board member—and funder—Marty Peretz, shared Ron's views and Howe was reluctant to antagonize Peretz.

Although hated by the left because of his book *The Rosenberg File*, which concluded that Julius Rosenberg had indeed been part of a Communist espionage effort and because of his writings against the Sandinistas, Radosh still thought of himself as a "social democrat." He was ambivalent about being situated in the "right-wing" camp where his critics on the left had effectively placed him by their constant vilification. Radosh had even voted for Bill Clinton in the '92 election.

I had no such ambivalence. The image of the right that the left had manufactured—authoritarian, bigoted, mean-spirited, neanderthal—was an absurd caricature that had no relation to the way I saw myself or my new colleagues after a decade long involvement along the political spectrum. Conservatism to me was liberal—a commitment to the values and principles of individual liberty embodied in the American founding. I had rejected the leveling illusions and totalitarian longings embodied in the socialist critique and had no apologies for what I had become. My only political regrets had to do with the durability of the political leftism that Radosh and I had once espoused and now rejected as dangerous and destructive. When Radosh alerted me to the appearance of Lind's article, the subtext of his call was a question: "Well, is Lind right about intellectual conservatism? Should you be having third thoughts?"

And so I regarded Lind as a sort of double who might reflect insights to me about myself. I also wanted to see how the intellectual world was going to treat him for his apostasy. When Peter and I publicly rejected half a lifetime of leftism, I was not prepared for what happened. I had expected the attacks from the left, that we would be smeared as "renegades," "CIA spokesmen" and worse. But only Peter foresaw the real punishments that were in store for us, in particular, the penalties the left would exact on our intellectual and literary careers. When Peter and I wrote our own declaration of independence in 1985 in an article in the *Washington Post* called "Lefties for Reagan,"† we had not been active in the Movement for nearly a decade. After our disillusionment, we had allowed a "decent interval" to elapse before re-entering the political arena and had not betrayed or exploited the confidences of recent friends. We thought the long gestation of our move to what we called "second thoughts" (a calculated but futile gesture to preserve our "independence") would pre-empt the attacks on us as "renegades" and "traitors." In this regard, we were naive.

During the ten years when we were not politically active, we had written a series of best-selling biographies and several celebrated magazine articles, some of which were optioned by Hollywood producers, and had carved out new careers as literary figures. But when our apostasy became public, the retribution was swift and seemingly without limit. Before our declaration, the biographies we had written were regularly given front page treatment in the Sunday *New York Times Book Review*, which described them as "hypnotically fascinating . . . irresistible" epics and the like, and put them on its list of the top ten books of the year. Once we openly discussed the reasons for our rejection of the left and admitted to voting for Ronald Reagan, however, all that changed. Our next biographies were relegated to the back of the *Book Review*, to be derisively dismissed. Despite our efforts not to be typed as political conservatives, we found that we were now unwelcome in the pages of the *Times*, the *Atlantic*, *Harper's*, the *New York Review of Books* and even the *New Republic*. Our first biography, *The Rockefellers*, had been nominated for a National Book Award. We now realized that as a consequence of leaving the left, we would never be in line for literary prizes again. Nor were the issues we raised in our apostasy the source of much attention or interest in these intellectual journals. We had been founders of the New Left, had written some of its basic political texts, and edited *Ramparts*, its flagship publication. Yet our defection was treated as venal in motive and our commitments dismissed by writers like Garry Wills (in *Time*) as "marginal" to the political movement of the Sixties we had helped to lead. None of the above-mentioned magazines took seriously the arguments that we and the other members of our group had raised at the "Second Thoughts" conference.

There was a further irony in all this, adding to my curiosity about the ultimate fate of the apostate Michael Lind. Perhaps no greater caution exists for a leftist tempted to leave the faith than the charge of "selling out." To those who make it, the radical commitment seems to be less a political than a moral choice. Leaving

---

† Included in *Deconstructing the Left* (Second Thoughts Books, 1995).

the faith is inconceivable to them, a sign that one is no longer a good person. Only pathological behavior—taking money or some other payoff—could explain to a leftist the decision to take a different political stance. To the progressive mind, no decent person could ever make such a choice in the absence of some kind of material bribe. Even in the post-Communist world, the average leftist remains in this way a vulgar Marxist despite all that has happened. The fact that Peter and I had actually *lost* opportunity for personal gain as a result of our change of heart made no impression on our former comrades, who accused us of selling out just the same.

The penalties we paid were a lesson for me in the pervasive control the Left exercised over the commanding heights of the culture. Lind's success in the aftermath of his *Dissent* piece now completed the instruction. Prior to his apostasy, Lind had been a nonentity in the conservative movement. He had no claim to importance other than the fact that he had been sponsored and befriended by conservatives who *were* important—intellectuals like William F. Buckley and Irving Kristol, hands that had fed him and that he now proceeded to bite. But once Lind did his about-face, this obscure junior editor of an obscure magazine (circulation 4,000), became an intellectual hot property. Whereas Peter and I had found ourselves unwelcome in the literary culture after our *Washington Post* piece, lead articles and cover stories by Lind now appeared within months of each other in the *New York Review of Books*, the *Atlantic*, *Harper's*, the *New York Times*, and the *Washington Post*. He was made a senior editor successively of *Harper's*, the *New Republic*, and the *New Yorker*, and was signed for three lucrative book deals, including an account of his apostasy, based on the *Dissent* article, called—what else—*Up From Conservatism: Why the Right Is Wrong for America*.

The transformation from right to left did pay off. In fact, it seemed less a conversion than a career move. Since Lind actually got all the benefits of conversion that my former comrades on the left had falsely attributed to Peter and me (without drawing any suspicion as to his motives), I was also curious in looking at his new book to see if he had gotten the goods as well as the goodies.

Up From Conservatism comes with a flap copy that misleadingly describes Lind as "a former rising star of the right" and a blurb from Gore Vidal comparing him to Tocqueville and describing the book as "a fascinating look—from the inside— at that web of foundations and other interested people, corporate and simply dotty, that now shape most of what passes for political commentary." Vidal, of course, means the Right, proceeding in his usual absurdist fashion as though liberal dominance of the culture and its media were a figment of those corporate and dotty imaginations.

My first interest, both in reading the *Dissent* article and the book, was the *cause* of Lind's break with the movement I had joined. It would provide an opportunity to check any new illusions that might have insinuated themselves into my political commitments. In writing our own *explications de vie*, Peter and I had been careful to point out that for us there were no sudden revelations on the road to Damascus, no single moment or event that unraveled the skein of our former political selves. It was our perspective that had changed and the change had been worked over many events in the course of many years before we arrived at the conclusions that were summarized in our book *Destructive Generation.*

If there was a single chain of events that encapsulated the process of our second thoughts, it was the war in Vietnam, which provided what we called the shaping "metaphor" for our generation's view of the world. It was the tormented aftermath of that war that became our point of no return. As the Soviets moved into the vacuum created by America's defeat, it was clear to us that the Cold War was a zero sum game. When America lost, so did humanity and the cause of freedom. Even in Vietnam. More people were killed in Indochina in the first three years of the Communist peace than had been killed in thirteen years of the anti-Communist war. These victims were a direct result of the "anti-war" movement's efforts. The survivors had been swallowed by a socialist police state even worse than the corrupt regimes that it replaced. To salt these wounds the left had demonstrated a lack of concern for the victims of Communist oppression after the war that was matched only by its continuing malice towards America itself. What finally turned us away from our former comrades was not merely the evil they had done, however, but their inability to look at their deeds and make a moral accounting, to steer an altered course that would keep them from committing similar acts of malevolence in the political future.

In *Up From Conservatism*, Michael Lind claims that unlike us, he actually did experience a Damascus-style revelation on the way to his new career. His epiphany came from the publication, in 1991, of a book called *The New World Order* by Pat Robertson, which retailed "a conspiracy theory blaming wars and revolutions on a secret cabal of Jewish bankers, Freemasons, Illuminati, atheists, and internationalists." Confronted with this "threat" from Robertson, who had founded a new and powerful organization called the Christian Coalition, "the leaders of intellectual conservatism—William F. Buckley, Jr., Irving Kristol, and Norman Podhoretz, instead of protesting, chose unilateral surrender." Intrepid souls who criticized Roberston, like Lind himself, were "denounced as 'liberals' and even 'Marxists.'" The result, according to Lind, was "an exodus of the major young intellectuals formerly associated with the right . . ." himself among them. The overall consequence of these events, in Lind's view, is that "American conservatism is dead . . . . Today the right is defined by Roberston, Buchanan, and the militia movement."

Someone who is not a liberal zealot or otherwise predisposed to hate and fear the right, or who is reasonably acquainted with American conservatives, might be tempted to close Lind's book right here with the statement of its thesis. The characterization is so irresponsibly off-the-wall, so—well—dotty, that further exploration of the author's thoughts seems hardly worth the exertion. Consider Lind's remark about an exodus of "the major young intellectuals" of the right following the surrender to Robertson. This "fact" adds a frisson of importance to his own departure and seems to support his claim about the death of conservatism. I did a double-take reading the sentence, since I had been unaware of any defection from the conservative ranks, prior to his own, although my personal interest in such a development would have been great.

Later in his text, Lind identifies "the major young intellectuals" as actually only three intellectuals: Jeffrey Herf, Bruce Bawer, and Jacob Heilbrunn. Herf was, in fact, one of the featured speakers at our Second Thoughts Conference in 1987 and is still a friend. It is news to me that Jeffrey Herf ever thought of himself as a conservative. At our conference he particularly outraged Hilton Kramer by defending some of what the New Left had done (while still strongly attacking its anti-Americanism) and by describing himself as a "feminist." Bruce Bawer is a book and film critic, who may or may not still be a conservative. The Free Press has just published a collection, edited by him, of what appear to be conservative gay viewpoints. Jacob Heilbrunn is a Harvard graduate student who was briefly at the *National Interest* and is known only for the article he wrote about Pat Robertson in the *New Republic* which he co-authored with Michael Lind. Some exodus.

As though aware of the indefensible nature of his central thesis, Lind repeats it endlessly throughout the book: "The 'right' now means the overlapping movements of the 'far right' . . . [p.7] The only movement on the right in the United States today that has any significant political influence is the far right [same page, same paragraph] . . . " Lind summarizes the philosophy of this right in the following words: "the fact remains that a common worldview animates both the followers of Pat Robertson and Pat Buchanan and the far-right extremists who bomb abortion clinics, murder federal marshals and country sheriffs, and blow up buildings and trains. That worldview is summed up by three letters: ZOG. ZOG stands for 'Zionist-Occupied Government,' the phrase used by far-right white supremacists, anti-Semites, and militia members for the federal government."

Nor is it just hateful philosophy they share. "In the manner of the southern right from the Civil War until the civil rights revolution, which operated both through the Democratic Party and the Ku Klux Klan, or the modern Irish Republican movement, with its party (Sinn Fein) and its terrorist branch (the IRA), the contemporary American far right has both public, political wings (the Christian Coalition and Project Rescue) and its covert, paramilitary, terrorist factions." Naturally, Lind doesn't name any of these "factions" or attempt to link terrorist and paramilitary groups with their alleged "fronts," like the Christian Coalition, which (unlike the IRA's front Sinn Fein) has *denounced* such violence. For Lind, whose book is an exercise in slander, the accusation is what counts.

How is it that William F. Buckley, who thirty years ago drummed anti-Semites and John Birchers out of the mainstream right and whose most recent book was an attack on anti-Semitism, or Norman Podhoretz, the watch-dog of Jewish probity and security, would surrender unilaterally to such hateful and menacing forces if they existed? Lind's answer is that Pat Robertson's Christian Coalition is electorally so powerful that conservatives like Buckley and neo-conservatives like Podhoretz are afraid to challenge him and thereby jeopardize the Republican agenda. Or, as an un-named *National Review* editor allegedly put it to Lind: "They're mad, but we need their votes."

The illogic of Lind's argument is breathtaking. If Robertson and Buchanan have identical worldviews (and such worldviews!) why would Robertson and the Christian Coalition support Robert Dole in the presidential primaries, as they did in 1996, and not Buchanan? Lind elsewhere in the book identifies Robertson as "the kingmaker" of the Republican Party. What does that mean if it doesn't mean the ability to determine the party's candidate? And if so, why not himself? If the far right is the only "significant political influence on the right" why didn't Robertson engineer his own nomination, or at least give it to a hard-core conservative like Phil Gramm or Bob Dornan? If fear of losing Robertson's votes was enough to intimidate Buckley, Podhoretz, and the neo-conservatives from confronting his alleged anti-Semitism, why were they so ready to jump on Pat Buchanan as an anti-Semite and even "fascist" (as the *American Spectator* and Bill Bennett called him), when he was winning 30 percent of the vote in two presidential primaries, about five times Robertson's own best effort?

It needs to be said, since Lind does not, that when Lind's original attacks on Roberston were taken up by the general media, Robertson responded publicly. Both in interviews and in paid advertisements in the *New York Times*—Robertson expressed his personal anguish and dismay at the implications that others had found in his works. He denied any intention to identify Jews as social conspirators, apologized to the Jewish community for any offense his book may have given, pointed out that nowhere in his book were the Jews explicitly singled out for blame, and recalled his longstanding efforts in behalf of Israel, which included marshalling crucial votes in Congress during the 1973 and 1990 Middle East wars, where

Israel's survival may be said to have hung in the balance. He concluded his *mea culpa* by declaring that he was proud to be a strong supporter and dependable friend of both Israel and the Jews. This testimony and the facts behind it—not fear—explain why Buckley and Podhoretz left Robertson relatively (but only relatively) unscathed while they were quick to descend on Buchanan (who refused even to consider that his own words might give anyone offense).

Robertson's behavior in explaining himself, it should be said, contrasts dramatically with that of other Israel-haters and anti-Semites, notably figures like Edward Said, Louis Farrakhan, and Gore Vidal, one of Lind's new friends, who once described Podhoretz and Midge Decter as "fifth columnists" for Israel. Farrakhan, unlike Robertson, actually preaches a virulent anti-Semitism to his flock and, moreover, has been embraced by forty congressional members of the party Lind has chosen for his new ideological homeland.

When he gets around to actually analyzing Robertson's text, Lind shows just how manipulative a guide he can be. In composing *The New World Order*, Robertson—or his researcher—did make an egregious decision to draw on tired conspiracy theories from anti-Semitic texts. But what is interesting about his use of those texts is that he removed most of their references to Jews, and particularly to the Jewishness of principals involved in the alleged conspiracies—a peculiar quirk, to say the least, for an anti-Semite, let alone for the kind of neo-Nazi menace that Lind has conjured. Nor is Lind unaware of this editorial process. Lind actually draws the reader's attention to it as though Robertson's omission of ethnic particulars is further evidence of his anti-Semitism: "Throughout *The New World Order*, as I shall show in further detail below, Robertson uses 'German' or 'European' where his anti-Semitic sources have 'Jewish'." Lind quotes a passage from Robertson's text and *inserts* in brackets the offending connections Roberston has removed:

> Later the European powers [i.e., bankers like the Rothschilds] began to see the wealth of North America as a great treasure, and some of them still wanted to get their tentacles into America's economy [note the octopus' metaphor, a staple of anti-Semitic and anti-capitalist rhetoric]. They eventually did so not by force, but by investing their money here, by sending people [i.e., Jewish bankers like Paul Warburg and Jacob Schiff], and by buying land.

This is a bizarre way to demonstrate that an author is anti-Semitic. The crucial questions to ask about what Lind terms "The Pat Roberston Scandal," are these: (1) Are Robertson's politics actually governed by these conspiratorial views (and if so how did he come to be an early supporter of Bob Dole)? (2) Are they shared by Ralph Reed, the director of the Christian Coalition, whom everybody, including his liberal opponents, agrees is a sophisticated political strategist and not a religious fanatic? (3) Are they shared by the one million eight hundred thousand members of the Christian Coalition, which as even Lind is forced to admit is a direct mail coalition and not a party or cult in the manner of the John Birch Society or the Nation of Islam? Lind makes no effort whatsoever to assemble evidence that would illuminate or answer these crucial questions, and thus ascertain whether Pat Robertson's conspiracy views are anything more than one man's hot air. In other words, Lind's "analysis" is completely devoid of any real world implications.

What Lind does do, for effect, is to lump Robertson with David Duke, who (unlike Robertson) was a card-carrying member of racist hate groups, and to assert, without argument or evidence, that the Christian Coalition is identical to the John Birch Society. Lind takes Buckley's unwillingness to attack Robertson (when he did denounce the Birchers) as an indication of the historic capitulation of mainstream conservatism to the anti-Semitic, racist far right. But the kooky doctrines of John Birch Society leader Robert Welch demonstrably infected his politics and that of his followers. Welch publicly attacked Dwight Eisenhower, a moderate Republican, as a Communist, and his acolytes followed suit. Lind does not mention a single occasion during the six years of the Christian Coalition's existence, that its policies have reflected a conspiratorial mentality or an "anti-ZOG" agenda. Buckley's failure to attack Robertson is the result of his judgement that Robertson is not an anti-Semite like the John Birchers

One section of this silly and sordid book that held a perverse fascination for me was Lind's effort to explain the world of intellectual conservatism, an environment with which I am quite familiar. Lind's chapter on the subject is called the "The Triangular Trade: How the Conservative Movement Works," and is as dishonestly constructed and argued as the rest of his book. Even, the descriptive phrase he adopts for his subject is a smear: "One might speak of the interaction of money, ideas, and activists on the right as a triangular trade,' like the Eighteenth Century cycle of rum-slaves-molasses."

According to Lind, the first leg of this "trade" is the "grass-roots" right, which he identifies as the Goldwater-YAF, right, linked via Lind's McCarthyesque sweeps to the John Birch society, *National Review*, and all the dread demons—the anti-Semites, the bigots, the militia storm troopers and killers of federal agents— he seems to invoke on every other page. The second leg in the trade is the "corporate right," which turns out to be the hoary specter of Wall Street and Big Business. The business elite, according to Lind, has "acquired its own intelligentsia in the form of libertarians," specifically the Cato Institute, which in Lind's fantasies draft all the tax-cuts-for-the-wealthy-legislation that incite the Gephardts and Boniors to their fits of egalitarian outrage. In sum, according to Lind: "The strategy of the modern Republican party is based on a division of labor, with the grass-roots right serving as an electoral coalition, and the libertarian right as a governing elite."

According to Lind, this arrangement presents a problem for Republicans, because the libertarians regard the grass-roots Goldwaterites as "fascists," while the Goldwater fascists regard the libertarians as betrayers of their authoritarian dreams. Making this alliance work requires an "umbrella ideology," which is provided by the third part of Lind's "triangular trade," the neo-conservative "brain trust," a network of intellectual think-tanks. The purpose of the think-tanks is to compel conservative intellectuals, through monetary bribes, to shill for the Republican agenda.

For the benefit of those who do not have any personal contact with the intellectual right, it may be useful to have some anecdotal light shed on this picture, which is as remote from the realities of contemporary conservatism as Pluto is from the sun. Thus, for example, Marshall Wittman, a former New Leftist and onetime head of the Waco Texas Free Angela Davis Committee, was until recently the legislative director of the Christian Coalition in Washington and thus in Lind's typology a crypto-fascist anti-Semite. Marshall, however, is a Jew. He is now at the Heritage Foundation, which is the biggest policy think-tank on the right, and actually the most influential in helping to formulate the Republican agenda. But the Heritage Foundation is not addressed at all in Lind's text (even though he worked there) because it is not libertarian and, therefore, completely refutes his thesis about how GOP policy is shaped.

Another friend, Shawn Steel, is a veteran of the Goldwater campaign, a former YAF-er, and a grassroots activist. He is treasurer of the California Republican Party and finance chair of Republican congressman Dana Rohrabacher's campaign organization. He is also on the board of the Center for the Study of Popular Culture, part of what Lind would call the neo-conservative "brain trust." Both Steel and Rohrabacher, on the other hand, are devout libertarians, farther from being "fascists" than any of my former comrades on the left including all of Lind's new friends. Both have been particularly active in recruiting Asian-Americans to the Republican cause. Neither, however, is unique. A reunion of Goldwater activists was held in Orange County during the presidential primaries four years ago, which I attended. Every significant right-wing Republican from the California congressional delegation and legislature was present to honor Howard Ahmanson, whom the *Los Angeles Times* has described as the "king of the religious right" in the state, but who opposed, for example, Prop. 187 (California's anti-illegal immigration initiative). Nearly every speaker (there were twenty-seven), led by far-right Representative "B-1 Bob" Dornan, supported the moderate George Bush over the far-right Pat Buchanan for president. So much for Lind's guide as to how the conservative movement works.

In fact Lind's analysis amounts to little more than the kind of crackpot conspiracy theory he ostentatiously derides. According to Lind, "The modern conservative brain trust originated in a scheme hatched in the 1970s by William E. Simon, Irving Kristol, and others." The plan was to make conservative intellectuals, hitherto an independent-minded, quirky, and diverse community, a controlled monolith that would function as the reliable tool of the Republican Party. "By the early 1990s, thanks to the success of the Simon-Kristol initiative, almost all major conservative magazines, think tanks, and even individual scholars had become dependent on money from a small number of conservative foundations." Lind has in mind the Olin, Bradley, and Scaife foundations. By this point, the puppet-masters Simon and Kristol are being referred to in Lind's text as the "Wall Street corporate raider" and "the ex-Communist-apparatchik." For the record, it is worth noting that Irving Kristol's connection to "Communism" is this: He spent a year in 1938 in a Trotskyist splinter group arguing with the apparatchiks and showing what a poor candidate for any Leninist Party he was.

Smears like this are not coincidental to Lind's argument, they *are* his argument. He writes: "The conservative movement these ex-radicals [like Kristol] crafted was therefore one that adopted the characteristic institutions and strategies of Communism while purveying an anti-Communist (not merely a non-Communist) message." The real Communist Party imposed conformity on its intellectuals through ideology and terror. Kristol's "party," according to Lind, imposes an identical uniformity through the dispensation of monies under the control of a few right-wing foundations. "What passes for intellectual conservatism is little more than the subsidized propaganda wing of the Republican Party. Public dissent on matters of concern to the U.S. business elite is not tolerated." †

This is pathetic and offensive rant. Joshua Muravchik and Ben Wattenberg, to name just two fellows at the American Enterprise Institute (AEI), signed a public ad supporting Bill Clinton in 1992, without suffering any consequences. Currently, there are at least three conflicting and hotly debated conservative positions on immigration reform, an issue of obvious concern to the business elite. In fact, the head of one conservative think tank has been hired by Silicon Valley computer firms to promote open immigration, while other "brain trust" members call for

---

†Recently, Lind has been invited to write for *National Review*, again proving that while conservatives may be masochists, they are not Leninists.

greater restrictions. Jack Kemp and Bill Bennett, whose Empower America qualifies as a unit of the "brain trust," flew to California to oppose Prop 187 in the midst of the election campaign, although Prop 187 was supported by the heads of all of California's conservative think-tanks. Almost every conservative journal has published internal debates on this issue.

Kristol, the grand puppet-master himself, is (correctly) described by Lind as censorious on cultural issues. But then Lind doesn't explain how it is that congressional Republicans have led the fight against the V-Chip and censorship on the Internet. The range of issues on which conservatives disagree is almost endless. *National Review* recently published a cover feature by Bill Buckley calling for the legalization of drugs, to the dismay of Bill Bennett and most of the conservative intellectual community, including the editorial board of *National Review*. An even more instructive incident took place over the publication of Dinesh D'Souza's *The End of Racism*. While the D'Souza book was funded in part by one of Lind's demonic right-wing foundations, it was publicly attacked (and severely damaged) by two foundation-funded conservative intellectuals and charter members of the "brain trust," Glenn Loury and Bob Woodson. So much for the party line.

Since Lind's strategy is reflexively one of tar and feather, D'Souza and Charles Murray get extra punishment as they have already been targets of particularly vicious liberal attacks. Murray is indisputably one of the leading social scientists in America but he and D'Souza are portrayed by Lind as intellectual whores—"subsidized conservative publicists"—hired to promote the political agendas of the Republican party. "If this seems too harsh a judgment," writes Lind, "suppose that Murray's research had convinced him that in fact Head Start programs did work, and needed to be substantially expanded—and that to do so he recommended higher income taxes on the rich. One need not be a complete cynic to think that he might have trouble getting grants in the future from conservative foundations, or renewing his stay at the American Enterprise Institute."

If complete cynicism is not required to follow Lind's argument, a dose of ideological blindness or just plain stupidity will help. How could anyone overlook the fact that Murray and D'Souza are best-selling authors and national celebrities who can command six-figure book contracts and lucrative speaking fees and thus are quite able to support themselves, in the unlikely event that AEI should decide to terminate them for such deviant views. In fact, Murray left another conservative think-tank and went to AEI precisely because the first did not want to support his work on the *Bell Curve*. AEI was willing to do so. So much for Lind's monolith.

As if Lind's penchant for the political gutter and disregard for the simple truth were not sufficient, when *Up From Conservatism* turns to a brief autobiographical moment, what is revealed is that Lind himself is a poseur, and a phony as well. The man who has exploited his minor league political metamorphosis for major personal gain reveals that he was never a conservative at all: "My political journey has been far less dramatic than a switch from left to right," he confesses midway through the book. "My political views have scarcely changed since college."

Astoundingly, given the hoopla that surrounded his "conversion," Lind's views, apparently, are those of a centrist Democrat whose political hero is Lyndon Baines Johnson. Notwithstanding this unswerving political allegiance, Lind insinuated himself into the conservative movement while still at Yale, accepted a job at *National Review*, and proceeded mole-like for ten years to burrow through conservative institutions—the Heritage Foundation, the Bush Administration, and ultimately the *National Interest*—taking advantage of the goodwill of conservative patrons all along the way, only to turn them—for personal gain—into the unlikely villains of his intellectually vapid, self-promoting tract.

Shortly after Peter Collier and I first entered the conservative world, I arranged a lunch with Norman Podhoretz who warned me: "When you were on the left, you got away with everything. Now that you're on the right, you'd better be careful, because they won't let you get away with anything." Michael Lind has made the reverse crossing. "Getting Away with Everything" would have been a good title for this reprehensible, gutter-sniping book.

Kara Hultgreen

Robert Stumpf

Paula Coughlin

Pat Schoeder

Sex in Combat

Tailhook Witch-Hunt[†]

According to Navy Lieutenant Paula Coughlin, a helicopter pilot and aide to Rear Admiral John W. Snyder, she had no idea that she would be walking into sexual hell around midnight on September 6, 1991, when she went up to the third floor of the Las Vegas Hilton to visit the hospitality suites at the Tailhook Association's annual convention. But as she entered the hallway of the hotel, she immediately found herself in a sea of leering male faces swollen with sexual energy. A taunting chant arose, "Admiral's aide! Admiral's aide!" A man bumped her from behind, grabbing both of her buttocks and lifting her up off the ground. Then, as she spun to confront this attacker, someone else grabbed her from behind. She felt hands going down the front of her blouse.

Paula Coughlin was not the only victim of this bacchanal. Ensign Elizabeth Warnick said that she entered a hotel room after an invitation and was immediately jumped by three naval aviators who grabbed and blindfolded her, threw her on the bed, and began ripping her clothes off. With heroic effort she managed to kick at the men, get herself free and escape from the room.

The scandal known as "Tailhook" which erupted two years ago, after Paula Coughlin told her story about what happened that night in Las Vegas, would eventually shake the American military and the culture that supports it more than any event since the trial of Lieutenant William Calley for the My Lai massacre two decades ago. Just as Calley's trial became a symbolic event for a military haunted by losing the war in Vietnam, so the Tailhook scandal was a symbolic moment for a profession still trying to accommodate to the requirements of a gender-integrated force. These requirements had already created a revolution inside the military, yet critics claimed that women still were "second class" participants, restricted from combat and thus from the careers that conferred the highest rank and esteem. When Tailhook, the annual convention and bash of the Navy's and Marine Corps' elite "top guns," seemed to have turned into an orgy of wholesale sexual harassment and assault it also appeared to have proven everything the critics said, presenting a picture of the male military culture that was not only resistant to change, but morally degenerate and out of control. When Navy brass instituted a "cover-up"

[†] This essay was written with the research assistance of Michael Kitchen.

in the wake of the revelations of Coughlin and other victims of Tailhook, it was taken as proof by politicians and the public at large of the existence of an Old Boy Network that would stop at nothing to protect its own. Critics of the military like Representative Patricia Schroeder said that heads would roll, and roll they did.

Two years and many military careers later, these images of sexual barbarism and cover-up are still firmly fixed in the American mind. Perhaps they always will be. But as the Tailhook investigations have been completed and the trials and court-martials of alleged criminals have begun, a very different picture of what took place that fall weekend is beginning to emerge. That the late evening hours of Friday and Saturday nights on the third floor of the Las Vegas Hilton constituted a mob scene which to some extent was out of control is beyond dispute. That some twenty-three thousand dollars worth of damage was done (albeit most of it the result of stains on carpets) cannot be doubted. That there was in fact public lewdness and sexuality, some drunken brawling, and a general groping of females by intoxicated military personnel has been proven. Some non-military women who strayed into the third floor party unsuspectingly were indeed verbally and physically abused and there were perhaps one or two cases of real sexual assault.

All this notwithstanding, the Pentagon investigation, conducted by civilian federal agents and involving several thousand interviews with witnesses and detailed reports on the night's activities in every single one of the twenty-six hospitality suites, shows something else as well: that many victims who were identified as victims in the press and even who are identified as victims in the Pentagon report, do not consider themselves victims; that many who do consider themselves victims, including the chief accuser, Paula Coughlin, were willing collaborators in the sexual frivolities that spilled over into the abuse of innocents; that when the party was over, and Coughlin and her cohorts appeared to advance a cause, it was not that of duty, honor, country, but a gender cause that sees the military as an enemy to be defeated by a war of social attrition.

From the beginning the Tailhook scandal had the air of a public burning rather than a dispassionate inquiry into the facts of the case. Before a single participant in Tailhook was given his day in court, the Secretary of the Navy and six admirals, including the commander in charge of the Navy's own investigation, had been sacked and had their careers terminated, four thousand Navy and Marine Corps promotions were held up, and the entire male enlisted corps was required to attend a million hours of sensitivity training.

The tangled chronology of investigation began with Paula Coughlin. She did not report her assault to the Hilton security staff or to the police the night it allegedly occurred, but the next morning she did file a complaint with Admiral

Snyder. After reading it, Snyder did not regard the complaint as warranting any action, a judgment that would cost him his career.

After several weeks without a response to her complaint, Coughlin wrote to Vice Admiral Richard M. Dunleavy, who notified his superior, Admiral Jerome Johnson, the Vice Chief of Naval Operations. On October 11, 1991, the head of the Tailhook Association sent a letter to squadron officers who had attended the bacchanal rebuking them for the excesses at the Hilton. "Let me relate just a few specifics to show how far across the line of responsible behavior we went," his letter said " . . . . We narrowly avoided a disaster when a 'pressed ham' (naked buttocks) pushed out an eighth floor window . . . finally, and definitely the most serious, was 'the Gauntlet' on the third floor. I have five separate reports of young ladies, several of whom had nothing to do with Tailhook, who were verbally abused, had drinks thrown on them, were physically abused, and were sexually molested."

This letter was leaked to the *San Diego Union* on October 29, triggering a full-scale inquiry by the Naval Investigative Service (NIS) producing the national scandal that has determined the dynamics and shaped the meaning of the case ever since.

Two thousand one hundred witnesses were summoned for questioning about Tailhook by agents of the NIS—one hundred more in fact than the number of those actually registered for the convention. Many were subjected to mandatory lie detector tests and other star chamber methods of interrogation that would not have been allowed under a civil investigation. And when this exhaustive dragnet identified only twenty-six assault victims, the small number was taken as a sign of the Navy's willingness to "whitewash" the problem.

A clamor went up from gender radicals demanding a larger body count. If four thousand men attended Tailhook, the reasoning went, there had to be more culprits. Summoning the Joint Chiefs before the House Armed Services Committee, longtime foe of the military Patricia Schroeder interrogated them in a voice dripping with sarcasm: "Is the bottom line [that] most of you think you could do without women?"

As a result of the pressure, the head of the Naval Investigative Service, Rear Admiral Duval Williams, was removed from his command. According to the subsequent Pentagon report, one of the admiral's sins was to comment, according to his female special assistant Marybel Batjer, "That, in his opinion, men simply do not want women in the military." His other two sins, according to the report, were his reluctance to interview admirals who had attended Tailhook and "his repeatedly expressed desire to terminate the investigation." A key testimony to this allegation was a female agent's claim that "Admiral Williams said that NIS did not have 'a fart's chance in a whirlwind' of solving this investigation."

Two days after the submission of the initial Navy Investigative Services Report, the Secretary of the Navy, whom the Navy report had failed to place at Tailhook even though he had been present on the third floor, was summarily cashiered.

Embarrassed by the Tailhook publicity and feeling itself vulnerable to increased budget cuts and the downsizing policy of the Bush Administration, the Pentagon brass simply capitulated to the pressure of powerful legislators, like Schroeder, who controlled its purse strings. On June 24, 1992, a second investigation was ordered, this time by the Pentagon.

Federal agents normally accustomed to tracking white collar crimes were dispatched by the Inspector General's Office of the Defense Department to investigate not only the Tailhook convention but the naval investigation itself. Their bottomline assignment was clear: to produce a more satisfactory result.

In this second effort, twenty-two hundred man-hours were allotted to the investigation of the first investigation alone. Instead of being criticized, the star chamber methods of the failed Navy investigation were intensified. Eight hundred more witnesses were interrogated. Immunity was given freely in exchange for incriminating testimony. At least one senior Marine officer was put on notice by investigators that if he did not cooperate he would be audited by the IRS (and subsequently was). Other officers were told if they did not comply, their names would be given to the media.

These techniques of intimidation paid off. This time ninety assault cases were identified, including eighty-three women and seven men. (These male assaults were the result of brawls.) Penalties assessed for these and other charges ranged from fines to dismissal from the service to possible prison terms. The ongoing inquiries have adversely affected more careers than any similar investigations since the 1950s. Like the McCarthy hearings of that era, they have created their own drama with their own heroes and villains. And as was the case then, the morality play also has a political text.

The heroine the media came to fix on was Lieutenant Paula Coughlin, aide to Rear Admiral John W. Snyder. Coughlin's complaint that she was sexually assaulted during the Saturday night revelries at the Las Vegas Hilton was the smoking gun that led to the investigations and the incident that dramatized the public scandal surrounding them.

On the same day that the Pentagon began its investigation, Coughlin surfaced on a television show, revealing herself ready and eager to step into the role of a military Anita Hill, and to play her part in the unfolding "rights" drama. In fact, the Hill-Thomas hearings had begun the very month of the Tailhook party and Anita Hill was—by Coughlin's own account—her role model and inspiration as she cast herself as scourge of the Navy. For its part, the press was more than willing to facilitate her new career as an icon of feminist courage and progress. Coughlin's name was soon enshrined in Women of the Year stories in the national media and canonized in feminist political circles. Commander Rosemary Mariner, a prominent feminist naval officer (and herself a lifetime member of the Tailhook Association) compared Coughlin to Rosa Parks, the pioneer of the black civil rights movement: "When one individual has the courage not to accept something that's wrong, it inspires other people to have the courage to stand up."

But like Anita Hill's story, Coughlin's has proven problematic, to say the least; a story whose hasty stitching begins to unravel under close scrutiny. In the same way that Hill's presentation of herself at the time of the hearings as a Bork conservative with no hidden political agendas has been effectively refuted by David Brock in *The Real Anita Hill,* Coughlin's presentation of herself as a morally outraged whistle blower with no ulterior motives in making her charge has been undetermined by the testimony (including her own) given to government interviewers.

Far from being an unsuspecting bystander who stumbled into the raunchy, raucous, intoxicated, and sometimes sexually explicit atmosphere on the Hilton's the third floor on the night of September 6, Coughlin was returning to a scene with which she was already familiar. She knew that the wild party was part of a tradition that went back more than a decade and she had been to Tailhook herself, six years earlier, in 1985. The sexual aggression she encountered this time was neither new nor unexpected. According to the Pentagon report: "Throughout the investigation, officers told us that Tailhook '91 was not significantly different from earlier conventions with respect to outrageous behavior." The report lists the Tailhook traditions that "deviated from the standards of behavior the nation expects of its military officers" including the Gauntlet, ballwalking (exposing the testicles), "sharking" (biting the buttocks), leg-shaving, mooning, streaking, and lewd sexual conduct.

Lieutenant Paula Coughlin was an active participant in at least two of these traditions—the Gauntlet and leg-shaving. Leg-shaving is described in the Pentagon report in these terms: "Most of the leg shaving activity at Tailhook '91 occurred in the VAW-110 suite. A banner measuring approximately ten feet long and two feet wide reading, FREE LEG SHAVES! was posted on the sliding doors of the VAW-110 suite in plain sight of large portions of the pool patio. According to the witnesses and the officers involved, the leg shaving was a rather elaborate ritual that included the use of hot towels and baby oil, as well as the massaging of the women's legs and feet. The entire process took between thirty and forty-five minutes per shave. Other activities often accompanied leg shaving. For example, officers in the VR-57 suite reportedly licked the females' legs with their tongues to ensure 'quality control.' Several witnesses observed nudity in conjunction with leg shaving. Three instances were reported where women exposed their breasts while being shaved in the VAW-110 suite. Witnesses related that some women wore only underwear or bikinis during leg shaving, or pulled up their shorts or underwear to expose the areas they wanted shaved."

Some of the women volunteers were strippers who bared their breasts and then demanded money to remove their underpants. "One uncorroborated witness reported seeing a female naval officer having her legs shaved while wearing her whites." That woman, according to one of the Tailhook defendants, was Lieutenant Paula Coughlin.

This accusation was made to the Pentagon team (which suppressed it) and to the press by Lieutenant Rolando Diaz, a Puerto Rican E-2C Hawkeye pilot. A sixteen year veteran, Diaz had been recently selected for promotion to Lieutenant Commander. Diaz had previously attended 'Tailhook '90 where he performed leg shaving without incident. For his 1991 leg shaving (he gave a "bikini cut"), Diaz has been charged by a courts-martial with disobeying the order of a superior commissioned officer who allegedly ordered him not to shave above the mid-thigh He has also been charged with conduct unbecoming an officer.

Diaz told the Pentagon investigators and the press that he shaved Coughlin's legs twice during Tailhook '91 in the VAW-I 10 suite. On Friday, September 6, Diaz claims he shaved Coughlin while in uniform and the next day—i.e., the day of her harassment—while she was in civilian clothes. Diaz did not ask any money for his service but requested that customers sign his banner. Diaz says that Coughlin signed the banner thus: "You make me see God. The Paulster."

The banner is now official evidence held by the Inspector General's Office. Diaz's attorney, Colonel Robert Rae has said that if needed, he will call in handwriting experts to identify Coughlin's script.

Diaz had reported this incident during his official interview with Pentagon investigator Special Agent Patricia Call. This part of his testimony was not included in Call's report. Similar omissions from the investigators' reports, damning to the male participants and protective of female participants were widespread, according to officers who were interviewed.

Paula Coughlin also participated in the Gauntlet, the most notorious Tailhook ritual. The earliest reported existence of the Gauntlet was contained in a Navy commander's testimony that he heard the term in the early 1980s, when it referred to the hallway outside the hospitality suites as it filled with drunken officers who had overflowed the rooms. Another officer thought "the practice started in 1983 but was not termed a Gauntlet until 1986." At this time Tailhook conventions were mainly stag affairs and as women walked through the hallway, officers would call out ratings of the women who passed through. A large proportion of the women who attended the earlier Tailhook conventions were groupies and prostitutes. Wives generally did not attend and the Las Vegas setting was treated as a port of call away from home. The Pentagon report notes that this was the first Tailhook after the Gulf War and was treated as a kind of victory celebration by the aviators.

One rationale for the Tailhook behavior, states the report, "that of returning heroes, emphasizes that naval aviation is among the most dangerous and stressful occupations in the world. During Desert Storm, for example, the US Navy suffered six fatalities, all of whom were aviation officers . . . Over thirty officers died in the one-year period following Tailhook '91 as a result of military aviation related accidents. Others were found to have died in nonmilitary plane accidents, in vehicle crashes and, in at least one incident by suicide "

As women were recruited to the armed services and became more of a presence at Tailhook, the behavior began to change and become even more sexual. According to the official report, touching was for the most part consensual and the women involved were "aware of and tolerant of the consequences of walking through a hallway lined with drunken male aviators." The aviators would loudly call out either "clear deck," "wave off," "foul deck" or "bolter," indicating the approach respectively of attractive females, unattractive ones, senior naval officers, or security personnel.

Any approaching females not turned away by these loud and raucous ratings would be warned of what lay ahead by another of the rituals associated with the antics of the Gauntlet —men pounding on the walls and chanting on their approach. Moreover, the dangers of a walk on this wild side were well known. According to the Pentagon report, "indecent assaults" dated back to at least the 1988 Tailhook convention. These assaults included breast, crotch, and buttocks feels and efforts to put squadron stickers on the "tail" areas of the women.

By 1991, these activities had clearly gotten out of hand. One female Navy lieutenant told the investigators that her squadron mates had warned her, " . . . Don't be on the third floor after 11:00 p.m." Apparently she disregarded their advice, because she told the investigators that between 10 p.m. and 10:30 p.m. on Saturday night the hallway was transformed from "a quiet place with twenty people" to "an absolute mob scene." On the other hand, the Pentagon report on this mob scene states:

"Our investigation revealed that many women freely and knowingly participated in Gauntlet activities. A significant number of witnesses reported that women went through the Gauntlet and seemed to enjoy the attention and interaction with the aviators. Those witnesses, both men and women, generally stated they could tell the women were enjoying themselves because, despite being grabbed and pushed along through the crowd, they were smiling and giggling. Some of the women were observed going repeatedly through the Gauntlet. Many women who went through the Gauntlet told us they did so willingly and were not offended by the men touching them."

Paula Coughlin was one woman who claimed to be offended, enough to go to her superiors and eventually the public, and whip up a national outrage against her male comrades-in-arms. Yet, as an attendee at Tailhook previously, she knew beforehand what the ritual entailed. Moreover, the evidence shows that she purposefully showed up on the third floor of the Hilton when the dangerous hours had begun.

That Saturday morning, Coughlin attended a Tailhook symposium at the Hilton, as Admiral Snyder's aide. In the evening, she went to the group's banquet wearing what she described to investigators as "a snazzy red silk dress" she had bought from Nieman Marcus. After dinner, according to her own testimony, she left the Hilton, went back to her own hotel (the Paddle Wheel), changed into a tube top, short denim skirt and "little black cowboy boots," and went back to the Hilton and up to the third floor where the hospitality suites were located and where sometime around 11:30 p.m., when she claims to have been assaulted, the Gauntlet was reaching its frenzied pitch

It is hard to believe that Paula Coughlin strayed into the hallway carnival unsuspectingly, or that she did not have a hidden agenda in putting herself into a situation where she knew she was going to be "harassed. "

According to Coughlin, as she entered the hallway, the men started chanting "Admiral's aide! Admiral's aide!" and Marine Corps Captain Gregory J. Bonam bumped into her from behind. "He grabbed both my buttocks and lifted me off the ground almost," she testified. She spun around and their faces were within six inches of each other. "What the fuck are you doing?" she asked him. She immediately noticed his eyes and his burnt orange shirt with the monogram "Boner" across the chest, she testified. Then somebody else grabbed her from behind, and Bonam forced his hands down the front of her blouse and squeezed her breasts. When Bonam let go, she turned and faced him. "He had his hands across his chest," she testified, "with his chest out proud and he smiled."

At the trial, Bonam denied assaulting Coughlin and testified that he had spent most of the evening out of the hallway in a suite nicknamed the "Rhino Room" in honor of his squadron's mascot. His attorney produced a photograph taken that night showing Bonam dressed in a green "Raging Rhino" shirt—not the orange shirt that Coughlin remembered.

Paula Coughlin was not the only "victim" with problems in sustaining her testimony in the legal proceedings. Ensign Elizabeth Warnick had accused Navy

Lieutenant Cole Cowden of holding her "down on a bed, pulling off her underwear, kissing her thighs and touching her pubic area," and attempting with two other officers to gang rape her.

Giving more detail, Warnick told the Pentagon investigators that she had a dinner date with Lieutenant Cowden and arrived at his room at 7:00 p.m.. The door was ajar, so she knocked and entered. As she stepped into the dimly lit room, three men grabbed and blindfolded her, threw her on the bed and began to take her clothes off. But she was able to kick one of them off and fight her way free from the other two and flee the room. She did not report the incident or talk about it to anyone.

The reason that she kept silent was that the story was made up, or embellished so as to transform its meaning. Under repeated interrogations, Warnick changed her story considerably. In the new version, she sat down on the bed with Cowden, who began to kiss her. She responded and they moved to more heated necking and she helped him take off her stockings. While they were on the bed she felt the presence of a second man and they began a "2 v. 1" (fighter lingo for a threesome). For a while, according to Warnick, it "felt good." Then she became uncomfortable and kicked Cowden off the bed and fled the room.

As it worked out, even this version of the story was false. Warnick's motive in lying, as she admitted under oath, was to deceive her fiancé and prevent him from knowing that she had cheated on him at Tailhook. Warnick had told investigators that she was disgusted with Tailhook after her experience at the previous convention. But under oath she admitted she had engaged in leg-shaving and allowed Cowden and others to drink 'belly shots" of liquor out of her navel and had had sex three times with a Lieutenant Commander (whom she also falsely accused of sexually harassing her). Excerpts from the transcript are revealing:

Defense Atty: Now, you indicated already that you lied on your initial account of having been assaulted?

Warnick: Yes, sir.

Defense Atty: You also indicated you lied about having sex with Lieutenant Commander X?

Warnick: Yes, sir.

Defense Atty: Initially, you denied having consensual sex with Lt. Cowden at Tailhook '90?

Warnick: Yes, sir.

Defense Atty: Is that a fair summary of your testimony?

Warnick: Yes, sir.

As a result of the exposure of Warnick's perjury, all charges against Cowden were dropped.

Far from being unique, the complicity of "victims" like Warnick and Coughlin were the rule at the Tailhook bacchanal, marking the ideological fault lines of the ensuing scandal as a witch-hunt driven by political agendas. The initial hysteria whipped by the politically correct winds of the time allowed vague accusations of "sexual harassment" to become imprinted as facts of "sexual assault" on the nation's pliant consciousness. But as the investigations have moved into various military courts, the flimsy evidentiary base has crumbled, producing a dissonance not unlike that which arose when Senator Joseph McCarthy would emerge from a Senate cloakroom claiming that there were two hundred and forty-seven or eighty-one or twenty-three Communist agents in the State Department, depending on who was asking and with how much specific knowledge. Thus press accounts of Tailhook will mention one hundred and seventy-five or one hundred and forty or eighty-three officers as having been involved in "assault" or "sexual misconduct" or 'conduct unbecoming" during the Las Vegas party, while the bottom line is—after nearly two years and four million dollars of investigations—the Pentagon has felt on solid enough ground to bring only three charges of assault.

There are really no surprises in this result, as the Pentagon's official report makes clear. There were, for example, one hundred Hilton security guards on duty during Tailhook and twelve present and patrolling on the third floor during the Gauntlet revelries where the scandal-making incidents occurred. The exhaustive summary of the Pentagon investigation lists and describes each intervention by the Hilton staff. The security officers "stopped three aviators from carrying off a wall lamp they had torn from a wall;' they "'broke up a large crowd of aviators who were chanting at a woman in an attempt to encourage the woman to expose her breasts;" they stopped an intoxicated naked male who had walked out of a room onto the pool patio and returned him to his room; they responded to incidents involving public urination, physical altercations, and aviators "expectorating ignited alcohol." In another incident, a security officer was walking with a woman on the pool patio when she was "grabbed on the buttocks." The report then states: "The woman verbally confronted her attacker but the security officer, at the woman's request, took no action."

The Pentagon summary then describes "the most significant incident reported by a security guard." Hearing a commotion, the security guards approached a crowd of men in the hallway and "witnessed a pair of pants being thrown up in the air." On closer examination they saw an intoxicated woman naked from the waist down lying on the floor of the hallway. The security officers assisted her and reported the incident to the Executive Director of the Tailhook Association, "warning him that improper conduct by attendees had to cease or the hotel would be forced to close down all activities in the hallway."

There was, in addition, an assault reported by two women who also reported the matter to the Las Vegas police. The police had referred them back to hotel security because the women refused to return to the third floor and attempt to identify their attackers. This was the only report of an assault made that night by any alleged victim either to hotel security or to the Las Vegas police "The security officers told us that, excluding the aforementioned incidents, no women reported being assaulted nor did any of the security officers witness any assaults."

Later, under pressure from Navy and Pentagon investigators, many participants at Tailhook claimed to have witnessed "indecent assaults," which were not reported at the time. In a section of the report titled "Victims," the claim is made that in the four days of Tailhook "at least ninety people were victims of some form of indecent assault," including eighty-three women and seven men. According to the report, sixty-eight of the assaults took place on Saturday evening, and, except for one, all of those took place on the third floor. The report adds the astonishing fact that ten of the women were assaulted at previous Tailhook conventions, eight were assaulted more than once, four on more than one occasion that evening, and that nine "did not consider themselves to be a victim," even though they had been subjected to indecent assault." In an intriguing footnote the report explains, "We have used the term 'victim' to describe any individual who was subjected to a nonconsensual indecent assault, even when the victim does not consider themselves victimized."

Lacking a real criminal dimension, the only way Tailhook could be made to appear an epoch-making scandal was to use the strictly military charge of "conduct unbecoming an officer" to inflate the number of total offenses into "one hundred and forty acts of assault and indecent conduct." But eventually, when it came time to prosecute, this method of raising the body count did not hold up in court.

Thus Lieutenant Cowden, alleged attacker of Ensign Warnick, was charged with "conduct unbecoming" on the basis of a picture the Inspector General's office found of him with his face pressed against a woman's breast. His tongue was sticking out and her hand was behind his neck, apparently pushing his head down. IG agent Peter Black tracked the woman down and interviewed her in Las Vegas. During the interview, the woman told agent Black that she did not consider herself to be a victim or to have been assaulted. She told Black that she did not want Cowden to get in trouble for the picture. Ignoring the woman's expressed views, Agent Black had her sign a statement that he wrote to include all the elements that would make a sexual assault case.

The cross examination at Cowden's court-martial proceedings revealed the lengths to which the government agents were prepared to go in order to produce culprits:

Defense Atty: That first statement by Ms. M., who wrote that?
Agent Black: I did, sir.
Defense Atty: Did she tell you that she didn't consider that an assault?
Agent Black: Yes, sir.
Defense Atty: Did she tell you that she didn't appreciate the government telling her whether or not she's been assaulted ?
Agent Black: That I don't remember, sir.
Defense Atty: You explained it to her that it was an assault whether or not she considered it to be an assault. Correct?
Agent Black: That's correct sir.

The Defense Attorney, Lieutenant Commander Jeffrey Good, then turned to the woman's own statement, producing an even more chilling look at the mentality of the government's agents:

Defense Atty: Have you read her subsequent statement that she provided?
Agent Black: Yes, sir.
Defense Atty: It's a lot different than her first statement.
Agent Black: Yes, sir.
Defense Atty: So, the statement that you wrote out [made it seem that Cowden's behavior] constituted an assault even though the woman clearly told you that she had not been assaulted ?
Agent Black: Yes, sir.
Defense Atty: Now, looking at the second statement, it's pretty clear that she hasn't been assaulted. Correct?
Agent Black: In her view, yes, sir.
Defense Atty: Whose view is important here, the view of the victim or the view of you?
Agent Black: Well, I would answer that question, sir, by saying that . . .
Defense Atty: No, the question was whose view is important. If you're talking about an assault, a woman has been assaulted, whose view is important?
Agent Black: In this instance, the government.

Thus, in the Tailhook investigation, it appears, the United States government has taken the position immortalized by Lavrenti Beria, the head of Stalin's secret police, who said, "You bring me the man, I'll find the crime." This of course is merely a particularly brutal way of expressing what has become the cardinal principle of the new feminist jurisprudence, which maintains that where gender is concerned, the crime is in the eye of the accuser, and, when the accuser won't accuse because of false consciousness or some other defect, it is in the eye of the government.

Almost as illuminating as the government's prosecution of Lieutenant Cowden was its failure to charge Lieutenant Diaz with "conduct unbecoming" for shaving the legs of Lieutenant Coughlin, an infraction he freely admits. Diaz is indeed facing a court-martial for leg-shaving but on a different legal ground. As the *San Diego Union* reported the story, "Rather than charge Diaz with conduct unbecoming an officer—a charge that might also have been made against Coughlin and the two other female officers identified by the Pentagon Inspector General as having had their legs shaved—the Navy took a different tack. Diaz was charged with disobeying an order from a Navy commander instructing him not to shave a woman's legs above the knees."

What the *Union* failed to add was that if such an order had indeed been given (Diaz denies that it was) it would itself have been an illegal order, since it had no bearing on military duties, and military orders must relate to military purposes. (You can't be ordered to mow a superior's lawn, let alone shave a leg below the thigh.)

Thus the charges based on "conduct unbecoming" reveal the political nature of the entire Tailhook prosecution. No charges of "conduct unbecoming" have been levelled at any females, even though culpable activities like leg-shaving, belly shots, and public sex could not have taken place without the willing participation of female officers. Lieutenant Elizabeth Warnick has not been charged with perjury nor faced with any disciplinary measures for lying under oath, let alone with any "conduct unbecoming" charges for her participation in belly shots and the "lewd behavior" which made her male partners culpable. Nor has Lieutenant Coughlin. Nor has any other female been faced with disciplinary action for levelling false charges or (as in the case of one female Navy lawyer) parading around the entire evening topless.

"The agenda of the Pentagon Inspector General did not include looking at the misconduct of women," a senior naval officer told *San Diego Union* reporter Greg Vistica, the journalist who broke the Tailhook story. "It was a conscious decision," the officer added, "to punish male aviators for misconduct. That was the direction, and investigators were not going to get sidetracked by the misconduct of women."

The Navy brass was going to try to appease the feminist attack by showing the nation that it would prosecute sexist men. As Acting Navy Secretary Sean O'Keefe said in unveiling the Pentagon report at a press conference on September 24: "I need to emphasize a very, very important message. We get it. We know that the larger issue is a cultural problem which has allowed demeaning behavior and attitudes toward women to exist within the Navy Department. Over the past two and a half months, the Navy Department has pursued an aggressive campaign to address this issue."

To prosecute the women involved in the Tailhook party would have been to puncture a fatal hole in the feminist myth driving the investigations in the first place—that all women on the third floor were victims. Before the appearance of the final report, Elaine Donnelly, a former Pentagon official and current head of the Center for Military Readiness, complained to the then Navy Secretary Dalton about the selective prosecution of male officers but received no redress. She later commented, "The apparent double standard at work here is both demoralizing to Navy men and demeaning to military women . . . I am disappointed . . . that you apparently have no intention of issuing a general statement of principle that prosecutions must be conducted fairly, without regard to rank or sex of the person who allegedly engaged in improper conduct at the Tailhook convention."

The reason for the Pentagon's disregard for the doctrine of fairness lies in the origins of the second investigation by the Pentagon's Inspector General, which was specifically tasked with finding out why the first Navy investigation didn't come up with the requisite number of criminals. Barbara Pope, an Assistant Secretary of the Navy, threatened to resign in the middle of the 1992 presidential election campaign unless all of the commanding and executive officers of squadrons who attended Tailhook were fired. Rather than stand up to this latter-day McCarthyism in which the officers would be assumed guilty before trial, Secretary of Defense Dick Cheney acquiesced to the Inspector General's witch-hunt, which would increase the body count of the Navy probe.

"I have been a Navy prosecutor, and I worked in the state's attorney office. I've been on both sides, but I have never seen the likes of this ever, anywhere," commented defense counsel Robert Rae of the suppression of evidence and extralegal methods used by the government investigators in their attempts to come up with a "body count" that would appease feminists like Barbara Pope and Pat Schroeder. "People are charged with felony offense-level charges with no evidence or evidence patently insufficient and totally without any credible testimony."

Commander Jeffrey Good, the lawyer for Lt. Cowden, concurred. "The reports of interview are shoddy and can't be relied on," he told the *Washington Times*. "I think Tailhook is a mountain out of a molehill from what I have seen. There certainly was some misconduct there, but I think it's been blown out of proportion and I think the Navy is overreacting with these prosecutions."

What Tailhook really represents is another skirmish on the most important battlefield of the new diversity. Until now, the military has been the only institution to remain immune from the malevolent influences of radical social reevaluations. But all that is changing.

The Pentagon report is fully aware of the culture war that enveloped its investigation. The report notes that the 1991 Tailhook convention was affected by the victory in the Gulf War, the downsizing of the military which would most affect the junior officers involved in the Tailhook excesses, and the growing debate initiated by ranking Armed Services Committee member Schroeder about women in combat. A GAO report, not mentioned in the Tailhook summary, estimated that 90 percent of the "sexual harassment" charges in the military as a whole stemmed from resentment over double standards and the role of women in previously male preserves.

The double standards present in the Tailhook investigations are, in fact, merely extensions of the double standards that have come to pervade the military in the last decade as a result of pressure from feminists like Schroeder. These range from double standards in performance tests at all the military academies except the Marines' to double standards in facing death. Women failed to be ready for battle at a rate three to four times that of men during Desert Storm (mainly as a result of pregnancy) and, in one notorious instance, 10 percent of the female sailors aboard the Navy ship Arcadia became pregnant after leaving port in California for the Gulf, thus avoiding the risks of actual combat. Not one of these women was courtmartialed.

This debate was in the air in Las Vegas in September, 1991. According to the testimony of one Navy commander, Lieutenant Paula Coughlin became embroiled in an argument with him on Friday night of Tailhook over just this subject. Coughlin, it was well known, was chafing under the restrictions that prevented her from piloting a combat helicopter. During the argument about women in combat, Coughlin angrily told the commander that "a woman getting pregnant was no different than a man breaking a leg." Five weeks before Tailhook, Paula Coughlin herself was lobbying on Capitol Hill for a repeal of the restriction on women in combat.

If Coughlin felt she didn't get the best of the argument on that Friday evening in Las Vegas, the subsequent scandal which her actions triggered changed the dynamics dramatically. In her new persona as a national heroine she told the *Los Angeles Times*: "I look at many of these guys—who still don't get it—and I think to myself: 'It was their Navy. It's soon going to be my generation's Navy.'"

Nor was the issue of women in combat only on Coughlin's mind at Tailhook, although she may have been the only one there who acted on her convictions. The conflict over the policy recently proposed by Congresswoman Schroeder and others to breach the wall barring women from combat by allowing them to fly combat aircraft was, according to the Pentagon investigation, "the single, most talked about topic" at the convention. At the "Red Flag Panel" of the convention where the issue of women flying combat aircraft was discussed, the issue "elicited strong reactions from attendees." These included cheers and applause when one male officer forcibly stated his personal objections to women in combat and complaints from the women when a male Vice Admiral failed to provide "sufficient support" for their position. One female aviator complained to Pentagon investigators that immediately following the Flag Panel, she was 'verbally harassed by male aviators who expressed to her their belief that women should not be employed in naval aviation. They also accused her of having sexual relations with senior officers while deployed on carrier assignment."

Instead of allowing this dispute to work itself out within the military community, with the possibility of restoring single standards for both genders and thereby eliminating much of the male resentment, the Tailhook scandal tipped the scales in favor of the feminists. In the wake of Tailhook, and the Clinton electoral victory, women were allowed to fly combat planes by an executive order of the new Secretary of Defense, a victory achieved by scandal rather than by demonstrated competence.

Meanwhile the trials continue. Symbolic of the tragedy of Tailhook is the case of Commander Robert Stumpf. An eighteen-year veteran in the military's most dangerous and demanding profession, he was Commander of the Blue Angels, the Navy's elite flight demonstration team. An F -18 pilot and Gulf war hero, Stumpf received the Distinguished Flying Cross for his heroism in Desert Storm. He came to Tailhook to receive the Estocin Award for the best fleet F-18 squadron in the Navy. But he found himself removed from his command without a single charge being filed against him. His crime was to have been in a private room (not on the third floor) in which, after he left, a stripper performed fellatio on an aviator. Commander Stumpf is like the thousands of victims of the witchhunt that scarred our country several decades past. But there is one difference. The vast majority of those who lost their jobs because of McCarthyism were supporters of a police state which was their country's enemy. The crime of Commander Stumpf was to serve his country and risk his life, as a male, to defend it.

Feminist Assault on the Military

For nearly two decades after the Sixties, the U.S. military remained the one institution that had withstood the baleful influences of the radical left. Now that the Cold War is over, this immunity appears to have ended. A series of relatively trivial incidents—a joke about women's sexual excuses, a skit with sexual innuendos mocking a female member of Congress—and a drunken party at which crotches were grabbed in a gantlet ritual, have triggered a national hysteria and a political witch-hunt that is threatening the very foundations of the military establishment.

Already, the witch-hunt has terminated or blighted the careers of a Secretary of the Navy, four admirals, a military aide to the president, and three "top gun" flight commanders. A question mark has been placed over the careers of thousands of naval and marine officers. And every male in the Navy judged guilty under the draconian law of the new puritanism *before* the fact has been condemned to eight hours of re-education in "sensitivity training" classes, designed—as in a latter-day Salem—to purify their souls.

The dimensions of what is happening are only dimly appreciated by the American public. The case of three-star Admiral John H. Fetterman Jr., a naval aviator with thirty-seven years of service, provides some clues. A family man with conservative moral values and a reputation for honesty and integrity, Fetterman had earned respect as the "people's Admiral," for his concern for the "little guy," and for his advocacy of a wider role for women in the Navy; Capping his long and distinguished career, he had headed the Navy's air forces in the Pacific before being appointed chief of naval education and training, the Navy's number one shore command. A month after the Tailhook revelations, Fetterman was busted in rank. Days later, he took an early retirement.

Fetterman's crime? He had been accused over a harassment "hotline" of shielding an aide from naval investigators. The aide, a chief petty officer, had made a pass, while drunk, at another enlisted man. In less fevered circumstances this incident might have slipped by without notice. But in the wake of Tailhook, the Furies of sexual purity demanded blood. (One female officer, among the hundreds who rallied to Fetterman's support, told the *San Diego Union* in horror, "They're going after the wrong admiral. This shows you the whole world is upside down.")

In justifying an otherwise incomprehensible act against one of its most respected commanders, the Navy hierarchy reached for the blunt instrument of innuendo. In an official statement, the Navy said that the relationship of Fetterman and his wife with the chief petty officer, "appears to have been unduly familiar." In a poignant defense to his commanding officer, Fetterman replied:

"That conclusion is based upon observations that my wife extended the courtesies of our home to the chief in question. In response, I must note my wife is a caring and gracious person. She has always made all members of the Navy family feel like they are part of our family. That particular attribute is one of her greatest strengths and one for which I will not apologize."

Then he warned that the measures being taken to root out sexual harassers might end up doing "irreparable damage to the military."

"For the past few months, we have seen the reputations of honorable men and women tarnished by innuendo, falsehood and rumor. Enough! Our Navy is populated by decent honest and dedicated people. They need to be recognized as such."

But it will be a long time before the Navy's honor is restored and the American concept of innocent until proven guilty is respected again in military quarters. The moment which has led to the current witch-hunt is far from spent. It began in earnest a decade ago, when the army attempted to introduce a sex-neutral system to test the physical strength of recruits. Designed to match individual abilities to military requirements, the Military Enlistment Physical Strength Capacity Test (MEPSCAT) provoked objections at the time from feminists inside and outside the military, who feared that sex-neutral standards might cause women to be barred from certain roles, particularly combat roles, which were the keys to military status and advancement.

Although the Air Force held out, and maintained the objectivity of the test, the Army and Navy caved in to their feminist critics. As the feminist objections were met, the MEPSCAT test was reduced to little more than a "guidance tool." The double standard had taken its first step in becoming a way of life in the military as it has in other institutions of American life. The only area where a true standard remained in force was combat itself. Now, ten years later, combat has become the issue, and with incidents like Tailhook ripe for exploitation, the pressure to surrender to the feminist levellers appears all but insurmountable.

That pressure is embodied in the "Schroeder Amendment," which would open the door to allow women to fly in combat. The Amendment is named after its sponsor, liberal Democrat Pat Schroeder, who appears to be the aspiring Senator McCarthy of the current investigative frenzy (*I have in my hand a list of harassers . . .*) In a July 9 letter to Defense Secretary Dick Cheney, Schroeder put the Pentagon on notice that "Tailhook'91 is a symptom of a larger problem" and that the resignation of Navy Secretary Garrett does not begin "to address the problem." To do just that, the

Congresswoman wants investigations and prosecutions that will enable the Navy to purge itself of sexual miscreants:

> "the Navy's inability to complete an accurate investigation and the failure to identity and prosecute the attackers . . . sends a clear message . . ."

In addition, Schroeder demands (and has succeeded in getting) re-education classes—"sexual harassment training [for] all personnel"—to cleanse the navy of existing bad attitudes.

Schroeder's bill to allow women in combat (which would also make women eligible for a future military draft) is the other face of the feminist juggernaut. It is seen by supporters as a"wedge measure that would lead to expanded combat roles and true institutional equality for women. A Presidential Commission has been appointed to review the issue and is scheduled to make a recommendation in November.

While the primary concern in making such a decision ought to be its possible impact on military capabilities, many of the advocates of change and many of those who will actually decide the issue have shown little interest in the maintenance of an effective defense. Schroeder, for example, was an anti-war activist before entering the House where. as a ranking member of the Armed Services Committee, she has been a longtime proponent of reductions in America's military posture. Serving alongside her on the Committee are feminist allies Beverly Byron (who has demanded that every officer merely present at Tailhook be thrown out of the service) and "anti-war" liberal Barbara Boxer. Another ranking Committee member and ardent Schroeder supporter is radical Congressman Ron Dellums, a recent camp follower of Fidel Castro and other U.S. adversaries, an opponent of U.S. military interventions over the last three decades who denounced the Carter White House as "evil" for opposing Soviet aggression in Afghanistan, and a legislator who every year has sponsored an alternative defense authorization bill mandating crippling cuts in America's military forces.

When New Left radicals, like myself, launched the movement against the war in Vietnam, we did not say we wanted the Communists to win—which we did—we said we wanted to give peace a chance; we wanted to bring the troops home. By persuading well-meaning Americans to take up our cause and by forcing Washington to bring the troops home, we accomplished our objective: the Communists won. With disastrous consequences for Vietnam and the world.

Examples of this kind of double agenda abound in the current feminist campaign and can be found in testimony before the Presidential Commission on the Assignment of Women in the Armed Forces. Dr. Maria Lepowsky, a graduate of Berkeley and an associate professor of anthropology and Women's Studies at the University of

Wisconsin, provided testimony in support of a combat role for women. Then Professor Lepowsky asked herself: "What would be some possible consequences . . . —if women were put in combat—on American cultural values and American society . . . ?" And then she answered her own question: "I think there might be increased concern about committing troops to combat, also perhaps a good thing . . . ."

In other words, Lepowsky was advocating that women be put in combat roles because to do so would make it more *difficult* to commit troops to combat! Such candor is unusual for the left.

The feminist movement, which supplies the ideological framework for witnesses like Professor Lepowsky and advocates like Pat Schroeder, is typical of those in which radicals have played significant roles. It is a coalition of different voices in which radicals set the political agendas and in which not all the agendas are on the surface.

Moderate feminists generally are seeking modest reforms in American society. Technological developments in the Twentieth Century have dramatically changed women's social roles. Women no longer risk death in the normal course of childbirth, and can choose whether to become pregnant or not. Together with labor saving devices in the home, which have reduced the demands of maintaining a household, these technological advances have freed women to consider careers in the world at large, including careers in the military, where they have historically made significant contributions.

Naturally these changing opportunities for women have required some adjustments in the culture, particularly since many of the developments occurred in a relatively short time span. The development of contraceptives alone, for example, would have been a catalyst of important changes. When women entered the work force in unprecedented numbers, attitudes had to be adjusted and laws had to be changed; some traditions had to be modified and others abandoned.

America is a remarkably open society, with remarkably responsive institutions, and these changes have taken place with consequent alacrity. And they are still taking place. The best and most constructive way for them to take place is deliberately, with careful consideration of possible consequences, and special respect for consequences that may be unforeseen. As the inhabitants of the former Soviet empire discovered, at great human cost, revolutionary cures can be much worse than the diseases they were prescribed for.

This is a lesson lost on feminism's radical wing whose ideology has been described by philosopher Christina Hoff Sommers as "gender feminism." (Sommers contrasts this with "equity feminism," a moderate position that really means getting a fair shake.)† When advocates of reform speak of "gender integration" of the military they are often invoking the ideas of the radical feminists without necessarily recogniz-

---

† Christina Hoff Sommers' *Who Stole Feminism?* (Simon & Schuster, 1994)

ing them for what they are.

Gender feminism is a bastard child of Marxism. It is the dominant ideology of Women's Studies in American universities and of feminist groups like the National Organization of Women. Gender feminism holds that women are not women by nature, but that patriarchal society has "constructed" or created them female so that men can oppress them. The system that creates females is called "gender-patriarchy." As the source of their oppression, it must be destroyed.

Radical feminists are social engineers in the same way that Communists are social engineers. They deny that there is a human nature, and they deny that there is a female nature, that human biology in any way fundamentally influences who or what we are. The solution to all social problems, conflicts, and disappointments in life is to manipulate laws and institutions so as to create liberated human beings who do not have prejudices, exhibit bad sexual manners, get into conflicts, or go to war. By changing institutions, especially powerful institutions like the military, and using their administrative power to brainwash people into adopting attitudes that are politically correct, these radicals believe that problems that have plagued mankind since the dawn of creation will be miraculously cured.

Social engineers like the gender feminists have little interest in questions of America's national security. This is not because they are in the pay of foreign powers, but because they believe that America is a patriarchal, sexist, racist oppressor and that its institutions must be destroyed and transformed beyond recognition, if women and other oppressed groups are to achieve their "liberation." Of course, the gender feminists are not so naive as to admit these radical agendas outside the ideological sanctuaries of Women's Studies departments. In testifying before presidential commissions they sound like moderates and equity feminists. They will say that placing women in combat positions is merely an extension of women working outside the home, and of expanding equal opportunity.

But placing women in harm's way and training them to kill is not a mere extension of working outside the home. There are, moreover, definite limits to equal rights and equal opportunity when biology is involved. Does an American male have a right to bear a child? Does he have an equal opportunity with women to do so? Do women have an equal aptitude for combat? Ninety percent of the individuals arrested for violent crimes in the United States are, and always have been, male. From this statistic alone it would be possible to conclude that males have a distinct advantage over females when it comes to mobilizing an existing instinct for aggression for the purposes of organized combat.

One of the leading military advocates of equal roles for women and men is Commander Rosemary Mariner, a nineteen year career naval officer. In June,

Commander Mariner testified before the Presidential Commission that women should not be excluded from combat because "separate is inherently unequal." Perhaps. But so what? The founding documents of this country recognize the rights to life, liberty, and the pursuit of happiness. They do not recognize the rights of short people to be tall, of less intelligent people to have higher intelligence, of less aggressive people to be more aggressive, of physically weaker people to be stronger, of men to bear children or of women to be deployed in military combat.

Men and women are different *and* unequal in various abilities. That, to all but gender feminists, is an obvious, indisputable fact. The question is, what are the consequences of that fact?

The difficulty in answering the question is the emotional element that is introduced into the discussion by the moral and political claims of the feminist left. Mariner's testimony before the Commission—a testimony infused with radical nostrums—is instructive:

> As with racial integration, the biggest problem confronting gender integration is not men or women, but bigotry. It is bigotry that is the root cause of racial and sexual harassment. From common verbal abuse to the criminal acts of a Tailhook debacle, sexual harassment will continue to be a major problem in the armed forces because the combat exclusion law and policies make women institutionally inferior.

The basic elements of the radical view are all here. Sexual relations between men and women are to be understood in terms of racial relations between blacks and whites. The problem of sexual harassment is analogous to racism and is unrelated to the different biologies and sexual drives of men and women. At the root of the problem are social institutions. "Tailhook '91," wrote Schroeder in her letter to the Secretary of Defense, "is the symptom of a larger problem: institutional bias against women." In feminist terms, the social construction of women that renders them different from men is made possible by a patriarchal system of institutions that causes them to be perceived as inferior. In the eyes of the gender feminists, the exclusion of women from combat is a keystone of this system. If women were to be included in combat (and thus treated as the equals they are), if gender roles were to be abolished, then sexual harassment would cease to be a "major problem."

Consider the proposition: For five thousand years of recorded history, men have been more aggressive sexually than women. Recognizing this, societies have universally established different (unequal) sexual rules for men and women. And for all that time, men (but not all men) have failed to heed those rules and have overstepped the boundaries of decent behavior. But according to the gender feminists, that is "merely" the past. Now the U. S. military has a chance to solve this problem once and for all. By passing the Schroeder amendment. By removing the barriers to women in combat. As soon as the "exclusion law" is changed, women's self-esteem will rise, men's respect for women will increase, and *mirabile dictu*, sexual harassment will cease.

It is difficult to believe that rational human beings could propose such nonsense, let alone a commander in the U.S. Navy or a U.S. congresswoman. But this is the fundamental idea that ideological feminists promote. And to which our military brass and political leadership are kowtowing at a frightening pace. It is an instructive example of how radical ideology, given the chance, can glue up the human brain. If anyone were seriously looking at the question of military effectiveness, they would see that the greatest threat to military morale today is being created by the onslaught of half-baked feminist ideas that are making every man Jack in the military—from the highest brass to the lowliest grunt—guilty before the fact, guilty just because he is a male.

Item: This summer†, Jerry Tuttle, a three-star Admiral who had been nominated by the President for one of the twelve top posts in the Navy, was subjected to public humiliation when the President was forced to withdraw his nomination. Why? Because a newsletter for which he was responsible printed the following joke: *Beer is better than women because beer never has a headache.*

Item: Three "top gun" flyers were relieved of their commands because of their participation in, or witnessing of, a privately shown skit in the annual Tom Cat Follies at an officers club at the Miramar Naval Station. A female captain complained the skit had sexual elements and lampooned Congresswoman Schroeder.

What is going on in America that a three star Admiral can be denied a promotion over a lame joke that he didn't even make? Or that seasoned flyers can have their careers terminated because of possible offense to a politician? How could a Republican president and Navy Department cave in to pressures like this, and why isn't there national outrage over the injustice and stupidity of it? And, finally, what is the problem with feminists who can't handle this kind of trivia? *And yet want to enter a war zone and engage in combat!*

There *is* a big problem out there and it is this: We are fast becoming a nation of hypocrites in our unseemly haste to humor ideological bluenoses like Mariner and Schroeder, and to submit the lives of honorable and dedicated men like Admiral Tuttle and the Miramar commanders to the tender mercies of the feminist thought-police.

Thanks to Representative Schroeder, her supporting wolfpack, and the weak-kneed military brass who won't stand up to them, the men in our armed services are now guilty for being men: for having encountered women who have used headaches as

† 1991.

an excuse for not wanting sex, for suffering the abuse of a vindictive congresswoman in silence, and for making lame jokes to ventilate their frustrations.

Anyone who suggests that it might not be a good idea to include women in combat has been put on notice by Commander Mariner and her supporters that they are, at the very least, encouraging bigotry and most likely bigots themselves. Studies conducted at West Point have identified one hundred and twenty physical differences between men and women that may bear on military requirements. Yet the U.S. Naval Academy has been criticized for not moving fast enough to increase its female enrollment on the grounds that this is mere prejudice. Senator Barbara Mikulski has demanded "an attitude change" at the Academy, and an official Committee on Women's Issues headed by Rear Admiral Virgil Hill has called for the "immediate dismissal of senior officers who question the role of women in the military." To question—*to question*—the role of women in the military is now regarded as bigotry by the military itself.

The word "bigot" has resonance. It is meant to invoke the specter of racism and, simultaneously, to appropriate the moral mantle of the civil rights movement for the feminist cause. This feminist attempt to hijack the civil rights movement is both spurious and offensive. Women, as a gender, were never oppressed as American blacks and their ancestors were oppressed. It is the big lie of feminism to speak of "patriarchy" as a system of oppression comparable to slavery, and to see women's restricted role in society as fundamentally unrelated to restrictions imposed by their biology and the economic environment.

Black people on the other hand were *enslaved* for centuries, their slavery justified by whites who judged them to be less than human. That was bigotry. That was racism. Before running water, before refrigeration, before antibiotics, before contraceptives, naturally the division of labor was more restrictive for women and their social roles were unequal. But technological advances, and the development of anti-biotics and contraceptives made change inevitable. *Sexism*, by contrast, is an inane and meaningless term invented by Marxist radicals and adopted by feminists to stigmatize their opponents. Its primary function aside from abuse, is to appropriate the moral legacy of the struggle against racism. No Western civilization, let alone western democracy, has ever regarded women as inferior beings in the sense that blacks were considered inferior. None has ever failed to value and cherish them.

Despite the fog of feminist propaganda we don't need elaborate studies to prove this. Men's feelings for women have been richly recorded in Western culture. Homer's *Iliad*, which gives expression to the informing myths of Hellenic society, and is a founding document of Western civilization, is about a war over a woman. Even the most dim-witted ideologue can see that there was power in womanhood even then.

Or to take more recent attitudes, anyone who thinks that before *The Feminine*

Mystique women in America were denigrated as mere bodies without character or brains should catch the next showing of any Katherine Hepburn film on the American Movie Classics channel. In *Adam's Rib*, to invoke one example, Hepburn and Spencer Tracy play husband and wife lawyers who wind up on opposite sides of a major case. Naturally, the wife wins the case and emerges as the more adult half of the partnership as well. Only in Betty Friedan's febrile imagination was the American family a "comfortable concentration camp" before the advent of NOW.

Yet the argument is still pressed that the decision to put women in combat is somehow crucial to women's self-esteem and to men's respect for women. It is a constant theme of the presidential hearings. In discussing the inclusion of women in combat, Professor Lepowsky had this to say: "There might be a significant impact . . . on female self-esteem, especially for young girls and young women, in the idea that male fraternity and male respect of women was possible."

On what planet is Professor Lepowsky living? Including women in combat would give women the idea that male friendship and respect for women was *possible?* If men don't respect women, why do women fall in love with men and marry them? Is there something wrong with women? Are they so brain deficient as to be involved intimately with a species that doesn't even respect them? Only a feminist ideologue could come up with such malicious lunacy, which only serves to confirm the suspicion that behind every radical feminist's concern for what women might be, lies a profound contempt for who they are.

And yet this is the kind of thinking that is being factored into the future of our armed forces.

What is truly worrying about all this is that there is now an atmosphere of intimidation in the public sphere that prevents any candor on these issues. Jobs can and are being lost, careers are being ruined, reputations tarnished because of politically incorrect views; because of bad attitudes; because the party line is not being observed. These are disgraceful times in America. And they are fraught with danger where national security matters are concerned.

In its Washington session in June, the Presidential Commission also heard testimony from William S. Lind, former defense advisor to Gary Hart. In his testimony, Lind referred to the suppression of information vital to the decisions the Commission was going to make. According to Lind, the Army Personnel Office had detailed information on problems encountered with women troops in Desert Storm, which had not been released to the public. They included the fact that the non-deployability rate for women in the Gulf was many times higher than that for men. Specifically, when the troops were called to battle, between three and four times as many women per enlisted personnel were unavailable for duty. The inability to deploy women troops caused an immediate turmoil with negative effects on unit cohesion, which is a primary component of combat effectiveness. If men deliberately injure themselves to avoid combat, they are court-martialed. But if women get themselves pregnant for the same reason they get medical leave and child support. Where is the equality in that? Another piece of important information not made public was the fact that despite rigid measures taken in the field, there was no drop in the pregnancy rate through the period of Gulf War deployment. (Pregnancy rates in the military are now 10-15 percent. Pregnancy during Desert Shield was the primary reason for non-deployability.)

Why is this information suppressed? Where are the famous investigative reporters from *60 Minutes* and the *Washington Post*, ever vigilant against the evils of military censorship? Perhaps a politically correct media lacks interest in information that could sow doubts about the case for "gender integration." Even if the suppression of that information might jeopardize our men on some future field of battle.

The suppression of information has provided one "answer" to the real problems that have developed in the gender integrated military. "Gender norming" has provided the other. "Gender norming" is the practice of institutionalizing double standards, so that women are measured in performance against other women, rather than men who can outperform them. "Gender norming" is now the rule at all military service academies. As is the cover-up of the adverse consequences of these policies.

The official position at West Point, for example, is that there have been *no* negative effects stemming from the admission of women to the Academy. The facts, as revealed in a recent Heritage study by Robert Knight, are quite different. Knight's information is drawn from the sworn testimony of a West Point official taken in a Virginia Court:

• When men and women are required to perform the same exercises, women's scores are "weighted" to compensate for their deficiencies.
• Women cadets take "comparable" training when they cannot meet the physical standards for male cadets.
• In load-bearing tasks, 50 percent of the women score below the bottom 5 percent of the men.
• Peer ratings have been eliminated because women were scoring too low.

To appease the heightened sensitivities of women in the present political atmosphere, even the men's training program has been downgraded:

• Cadets no longer train in combat boots because women were experiencing higher rates of injury.
• Running with heavy weapons has been eliminated because it is "unrealistic and therefore inappropriate" to expect women to do it.
• The famed "recondo" endurance week during which cadets used to march

with full backpacks and undergo other strenuous activities has been eliminated, as have upper-body strength events in the obstacle course.

It is one thing to have second-rate professors in the humanities because of affirmative action quotas that lower standards. But a second rate officer corps?

Not surprisingly, resentment on the part of male cadets is high. One indication is that more than 50 percent of the women cadets at West Point reported that they had been sexually harassed last year.

It is a perfectly sinister combination. Rub men's noses in arbitrariness and unfairness, and then charge them with sexual harassment when they react. It is also a perfect prescription for accumulating power and controlling resources. Which is what this witchhunt—no different in this regard from any other—is ultimately about. For every male who falls from grace because he is suspected of sexual harassment, or of defending standards that may be unfavorable to women, or of not reacting strongly enough to sexual harassment, there is a politically correct career officer or politician ready to take advantage of his misfortune. Rosemary Mariner is a candidate for admiral; Beverly Byron has been mentioned as a possible Secretary of the Navy; Pat Schroeder has her sights on a cabinet post, perhaps Secretary of Defense.

Who is going to pay the price for these ambitions on the field of battle?

This brings us to another problem raised by William Lind, which is that of unit cohesion and combat effectiveness. In combat men will act to protect women and this will undermine the effectiveness of the unit. The male soldier's protective instinct is heightened by his knowledge of what the male enemy will do to females taken prisoner of war. This is not mere theory. The Israelis, who pioneered the introduction of women in combat during their War of Liberation, now bar women from such roles. They found that "if you put women in combat with men, the men immediately forget about their tactical objective and they move instead to protect the women."

The Israelis abandoned the practice of putting women into combat positions because it weakened their forces and exposed their fighting men to even greater risks. Should Americans repeat the Israelis' mistake just to humor the feminist left?

No amount of sensitivity training, no amount of brainwashing can alter human nature. The Communists proved that at unbelievable cost. They could not make a new socialist man (or woman) who would be cooperative and not competitive under a social plan, who would respond as effectively and efficiently to administrative commands as they had to market incentives, who would be Communist and not individualist.

The Communists killed tens of millions of people and impoverished whole nations trying to change human nature, all the time calling it "liberation," just as radical feminists do. It didn't work. Social experiments that disregard fundamental human realities in the name of abstract pieties will always fail. But they will cause incalculable social damage and irreparable human suffering before they collapse.

And yet, under the guidance of feminist social engineers, our newly sensitized military leadership marches on. The Air Force has established a SERE program (Survival, Evasion, Resistance, and Escape), including its own "prisoner of war" camp in the state of Washington to desensitize its male recruits so that they won't react like men when female prisoners are tortured. In other words, in their infinite wisdom, Ms. Schroeder and her feminist allies have enlisted the military in a program to brainwash men so that they won't care what happens to women. That's progress and social enlightenment, feminist style.

Of course, it is not necessary to gain access to the information that the military has suppressed or to be familiar with military terms like "unit cohesion" to see that America's war-making ability has already been weakened by the decision to deploy large numbers of women on battlefields overseas, even absent a combat role. Who does not remember the poignant stories which the networks elaborated in lavish detail about the children left behind by their mothers on duty in the Persian Gulf? And in some cases mothers and fathers. (In fact there were sixteen thousand three hundred and thirty-seven single military parents and one thousand two hundred and thirty-one military couples, who left anxious children behind during the Gulf War.) In the irresponsibly gifted hands of network reporters, even the family pets orphaned by their owners became objects of national concern. And for some, occasions to oppose the war.

The net result is that an American president now is under pressure to win a war in four days or risk losing the war at home. How many dictators are going to test the will of America's liberated military and compassionate citizenry in future conflicts? These changes have implications for diplomacy and long term national security that are literally incalculable. Yet Schroeder and Co. want them decided on the basis of cheap and empty slogans like "separate is inherently unequal."

In the summer of 1992, the military establishment has acted with cowardice to the all-out assault on America's armed services by Congresswomen Schroeder, Byron, Boxer, Mikulski et al. In the reigning atmosphere of political intimidation, even an offending skit could send career servicemen to the stake. Among the public figures lampooned in the Tom Cat Follies were President Bush and Vice President Quayle. But it was a rhyme about Representative Pat Schroeder that sent the Navy brass into paroxysms of fear and scrambling for a sword to fall on. When the smoke cleared, three dedicated careers were in the tank because of this nonsense. Three careers destroyed as a result of Navy hypocrisy and fear of the wrath of one bigoted U.S. congresswoman. When the history of this sorry episode is written, maybe someone will call it the Feline Follies.

One might well ask, what qualifies someone like Pat Schroeder to intimidate the entire American military establishment and to shape its destiny through the next generation? During the cold war Pat Schroeder and her supporters in the Congressional left worked overtime to hobble and disarm America in the face of the Soviet threat. In 1981, when Soviet armies were spreading death and destruction across Afghanistan and the United States had boycotted the Olympics in order to isolate the Soviet aggressor, Pat Schroeder and a group of left-wing House members hosted a delegation from the World Peace Council, a Soviet propaganda front, providing a KGB operation with a forum in the halls of Congress.

In 1982, with Soviet armies occupying Afghanistan, with fifty thousand Cuban troops waging civil war in Ethiopia and Angola, with a Communist base established on the American mainland, with a Communist insurgency raging in El Salvador, with thousands of nuclear warheads in Central Europe and Warsaw Pact forces outnumbering NATO troops by a two to one margin, Congresswoman Schroeder proposed an amendment to reduce the number of U.S. military personnel stationed overseas *by half* (HR 6030). If ever a member of the U.S. Government proposed a prescription for national suicide, this was it. Fortunately, three hundred and fourteen Democrats joined Republicans in defeating Schroeder's amendment on the floor.

In the *Congressional Quarterly*, Pat Schroeder is noted for her efforts against nuclear testing while the Soviets were still our adversaries, against further development of the MX missile, against proposed funding levels for the Strategic Defense Initiative and the B-2 bomber—and against authorizing the President to use force to stop Saddam Hussein.

Maybe Ms. Schroeder's Denver constituents approve of the attitudes these positions reflect. For most Americans however, Pat Schroeder's credentials on issues of national defense should be cause for alarm.

The military is the one American institution that survived the Sixties intact. Now it threatens to become a casualty of current radical fashions. Of far more concern than any possible injustice that might be associated with the exclusion of women from combat is the assault on the military that is now being conducted in the name of "gender integration," the elimination of sexual harassment, and the purging of male bigots. The worst crimes of our century have been committed by idealists attempting to eradicate just such "injustices," stamp out politically incorrect attitudes and reconstruct human nature. Let's not add the weakening of America's military to the depressing list of disasters of these utopias that failed.†

---

† The Presidential Commission decided not to recommend the assignment of women to combat but the following year Bill Clinton was elected and his Administration decided to ignore the recommendation and introduce women into combat roles.

Pilot B

Almost everyone knows about the sex scandal brewing in the army, which currently involves seven officers at the Aberdeen Proving Grounds. The officers are accused of sexual abuses against females under their command, which include charges of rape, sodomy, and assault. But until the NAACP stepped into the case a week ago, very people were aware that all seven officers are black, while most of their alleged female victims are white. Both the sex scandal and the racial coverup are products of political correctness run amuck—a current of radical mischief that many thought was yesterday's news, but which is still running so strong as to threaten the efficacy of the one institution that previously appeared impervious to such assaults.

The attack is being mounted under the banner of "de-sexegrating" the military (the term belongs to former congresswoman and long-time anti-military activist Patricia Schroeder who has led the crusade). The idea is to put women in combat and combat-support roles once reserved for men, as though the problems associated with such an agenda were trivial and the rationale for previous male prominence no different than the rationale used by white supremacists to preserve their privileges in the segregationist south.

Now that the NAACP has stepped into the Aberdeen case, however, it appears that the facts are not so simple. Five women "victims" have stepped forward to confess that they were not raped or abused. They have accused military investigators, eager to show that the Army was ready to deal with sexual harassers, of putting words into their mouths and threatening them with punishment for the consensual sex that did take place unless they filed serious criminal charges against the men.†

This scenario exactly parallels the infamous Tailhook case. The government was never able to get a single conviction of the Tailhook defendants because the women "victims" under cross examination in court admitted to having had consensual sex. They told similar stories of military investigators threatening them and putting words in their mouths in order that the top military brass might appear politically correct. Even the celebrated Paula Coughlin, whose civil suit against the Hilton Hotel was eventually successful, was shown to have been a willing participant in the Tailhook sexcapades. These facts are not well known, because the white males accused did not have an NAACP to intervene in their behalf. Without the

---

† The most prominent of the accused figures, Gene McKinney, Sergeant Major of the Army, faced fifty-five years for his alleged crimes. He was acquitted of all eighteen sexual charges however, after the Monica Lewinsky scandal, and while the President's poll ratings were over 60 percent, which would have made it difficult for any jury to demand serious punishment for such alleged behavior.

race card to trump the gender card, they were hung out to dry.

The national hysteria over Tailhook, whipped up by the feminist left, resulted in the most extensive witch-hunt in American history, ending the careers of hundreds of seasoned officers, admirals of flag rank, and war heroes, many of whom were not even at Tailhook or did not participate in its celebrated events. The pressure to destroy the "male culture" of the military led to more lost careers than were destroyed by Joseph McCarthy and a crisis in military morale which has decimated the ranks of seasoned officers. At least one female navy pilot, Kara Hultgreen, is also dead as a result.

Hultgreen was a Navy pilot who would have been grounded before her death had she been a man and held to normal navy standards of competence. But the pressure from feminist politicians in Washington, led by Schroeder, then ranking member of the Armed Services Committee, was so intense in its demand that the Navy qualify females to fly combat planes like the F-14, that normal standards were thrown overboard and Hultgreen's training continued despite her inadequacies. Pushed beyond her ability, Hultgreen crashed her forty million dollar plane into the sea. In the wake of this tragedy, the press has played politically correct coverup for the feminists and the Navy. No attempt of course has been made to assess the military and financial consequences of the de-sexegration agenda, or its suspect sources.

Schroeder is a left-wing Democrat, whose entire career could be viewed as an assault on America's defense establishment. She entered congress in 1974, pledging to cut off all military aid to Cambodia and South Vietnam. The aid was cut, the anti-Communist regimes fell, and two million Indochinese were slaughtered in the bloodbaths that followed. Ms. Schroeder escaped judgment for this catastrophe, and went on to oppose every subsequent use of American military power over the next twenty-years, right up to the war in the Persian Gulf. Fortunately, she belonged to the party out of power, and Republican presidents, with the assist of a battalion of "boll-weevil" Democrats, were able to maintain America's military posture adequately and to sustain the standards that had kept America's fighting force the best in the world.

During the Bush Administration, a Presidential Commission on the Assignment of Women in the Armed Forces was convened which specifically recommended that women not be assigned to combat for reasons that lie at the heart of the above-mentioned incidents. Four years ago, however, the American people elected William Jefferson Clinton as their commander-in-chief and the policy of the military in the contested area of women in combat changed. With Clinton in the White House, the Schroederites resumed their agenda, disregarding the recommendations of the presidential commission. The death of Kara Hultgreen is one result; the sexual fiasco at Aberdeen is another.

A third is a lawsuit that has been filed by a Schroeder-sponsored group called

WANDAS (Women Active In the Nation's Defense and Their Advocates and Supporters) against a think tank and two metropolitan newspapers who had the temerity to challenge this mind-set. The Center for Military Readiness is a public interest group concerned about the impact of ill-considered feminist ideology on military effectiveness. Its head, Elaine Donnelly, was a member of the presidential commission. When journalists at the *San Diego Union* and *Washington Times* reported Donnelly's charges that in the wake of Hultgreen's death the military was preparing to qualify a second unqualified female flyer (known as "Pilot B"), WANDAS went on the attack, suing both papers and Donnelly.

The suit against Donnelly and the two papers is a naked attempt to silence critics of Pat Schroeder's de-sexegration crusade. The crusade has already convinced the Army's chief officer, General Reimer, that the military can be "de-sexualized." Perhaps only another military mind could comprehend this. It requires two million dollars each to train pilots like Kara Hultgreen and "Pilot B." Pilot B is no longer flying any planes. Last year she became pregnant and is now the mother of a new baby daughter.

Steven & Abigail Thernstrom

Ward Connerly

Geronimo Pratt

Lino Graglia

Ethnic Mix

Dialogue on Race

I n an editorial comment on the Clinton race initiative, a *New York Times* reporter called it "The Honest Dialogue That Is Neither." The *Times*' explanation for this masquerade was that blacks were not participating frankly in the dialogue because they know that if they charged whites with racism "that sort of bluntness would end the conversation." Whites on the other hand, do not "want to talk openly about their suspicions that blacks may be genetically inferior."

Far from explaining why Clinton's dialogue cannot get off the ground, this liberal "analysis" merely adds fuel to the already existing racial fire. Clinton liberals think that the problem is white racism, and therefore their idea of a dialogue is for blacks to express their anger at a status quo that denies them equality, and for whites who are in denial about this reality to come to their senses and express their contrition. That is why Clinton has stacked his race commission with racial leftists, like John Hope Franklin and Angela Oh. That is why his racial leftists excluded opponents of affirmative action, like Ward Connerly, from their initial public forum. That is why when Clinton invited another opponent of racial preferences, Abigail Thernstrom, to his own "town meeting," he did so solely for the purpose of bullying her into submission. Her role was to be a white Sister Souljah:

"Abigail, do you favor the U.S. Army abolishing the affirmative action program that produced Colin Powell? Yes or no?"

Abigail stuttered an answer that she didn't think affirmative action preferences were responsible for Powell's success. Clinton slapped her down with the retort that Colin Powell himself thinks it was. But Colin Powell is on record saying that his success was not owed to affirmative action, while the U.S. Army has no affirmative action program for blacks of the kind opposed by Connerly and Thernstrom. The army has no set asides, no rigged racial standards (no lesser number of push-ups required or targets hit) and therefore no astronomical drop-out rates after admission of under-qualified blacks as the objectionable affirmative action programs do.

The Connerly and Thernstrom episodes underscore that, in the liberal view, there is really only one side of this issue as far as anyone who is a decent human being is concerned, and the liberals own it. Perhaps that is why every authority cited in the *Times*' article—Michael Eric Dyson, Roger Wilkins, Andrew Hacker, and

Orlando Patterson, occupies the left side of the political spectrum and supports affirmative action policies.

The reason there won't be a dialogue on race this season is not because there is only one reasonable, moral side to the question, but because liberals are unable to face the fact that there are more than one. Liberals are in a state of profound denial of the realities that fuel the racial debate. Bluntly, these are (1) the current failure of blacks and other select minorities to meet the standards that have been set for everyone else; and (2) a subtext of anti-white racism, which allows the white community and its alleged prejudices to be made the scapegoat for this failure.

An example of this denial was on display in the same day's issue of the *Los Angeles Times*, where long-time leftwing civil rights activist Roger Wilkins described the "essence" of the position taken by opponents of affirmative action as the fact "that the civil-rights movements of the 1950s and '60s left us with a degree of racism so negligible that the only things now threatening our racial tranquility are race-conscious remedies, particularly affirmative action."

To disabuse these opponents of their complacency, Wilkins reminds us that "real gaps in income, wealth, education, health, housing opportunities and employment still remain, at all education levels, and are especially acute for the least skilled. And, tragically, more than 40 percent of black children are growing up in poverty." This is the essence of liberal thinking. If there is a gap between blacks and whites which is detrimental to blacks, then whites must be responsible. To think differently would be to "blame the victim." But the facts show otherwise. Fully 85 percent of black children who are poor are living in single parent families. Statistics show that six out of seven children raised by single mothers will be poor regardless of race. There is no racially induced gap once the actual behavior of blacks is taken into account. The same can be said for virtually every other disparity regularly trotted out by liberals to show the lingering "institutional racism," that is alleged to be responsible for the failure of some blacks to climb the American ladder of success.

These are the realities that liberals cannot face: Blacks are under-represented at elite universities because their test scores are abysmal compared to most other groups. Blacks are incarcerated in prisons in staggering numbers because they commit crimes out of all proportion to their representation in the population. Those blacks who are chronically unemployed, are unemployed not because there are no jobs, nor because they are barred from jobs by their skin color. Chronically unemployed blacks, concentrated in our inner cities, are disproportionately unemployed because they are disproportionately unemployable: they do not seek work as avidly as other groups do; they make their neighborhoods too dangerous for businesses to establish operations; they refuse jobs that offer only "chump change," and prefer criminal activities to honest employment; and they do not acquire the educational skills or the work habits of discipline, punctuality, and reliability necessary for them to be worth employing.

These are hard truths, but they need to be faced if the black underclass is going to take advantage of the same opportunities that a thriving black middle class has already embraced. Liberals do not want to hear this. They will attack those who articulate these facts as "racists" in order to silence them. They will not invite them to their "town hall" meetings, and if they do it will only be to clobber them into submission or paint them as moral pariahs. And that is the bottom-line reason why Clinton's initiative, for now, is only a dialogue of the deaf.

Pork-Barrel Racism

A Clinton Task-Force has unanimously recommended against adding the category "multiracial" to the government census forms which now list four official "races": white, black, American Indian and Alaskan Native, Asian and Pacific Islander. According to a *Los Angeles Times* report on this development, "The recommendation marks a victory for traditional civil rights and ethnic advocacy groups, including the NAACP and the National Council of La Raza, which were pitted against the newer multiracial advocacy groups." Welcome to the Alice-in-Wonderland world of the new American apartheid.

Asians are not a race, nor is the NAACP an ethnic advocacy group (it is a group concerned about a race). The National Council of La Raza (The Race) *is* an ethnic advocacy group, but neither "Hispanic" nor "Latino"—the ethnic constituencies it claims to represent—are actual ethnicities. They are language groups, but in the case of "Latinos" not even that. Moreover, the terms "Latino" and "Hispanic" cover not only different but polarized ethnicities, nationalities and races (e.g., the "Mexican" Indians of Chiapas and their European-descended oppressors). Finally, neither the NAACP or La Raza, described as "civil rights" groups, can be said to be much concerned for civil rights, judging by their advocacy of racial and ethnic preferences and the zeal with which they have opposed the civil rights claims of multiracial Americans in this case.

As the multiracial latecomers have discovered, there is no room for them at the "civil rights" table. Despite creating their own advocacy institutions modeled on what's become of the civil rights struggle, including a "march on Washington" to protest their "under-representation," they have come up virtually empty in their quest for a census box. For now, there is not going to be a Tiger Woods band in the

American rainbow. No designation for the one-quarter white, one-eighth black, one-quarter Thai, one-quarter Chinese, one-eighth Indian American sports hero.

Of course, the Administration liberals didn't neglect to throw a crumb in their direction, namely, the ability to check off multiple boxes if they should so choose. A spokesperson for the multiracial crowd named Susan Graham, who is president of a group called "Project Race" (in America! in 1997!), welcomed the victory, but insisted that her troops would continue to pursue the "multiracial" category: "As it is, my children cannot be multiracial children. My children can be 'check-all-that-apply' children and I do not consider that fair."

Well, it's not really about fairness Susan. It's about a racial/ethnic (check-one-of-the-above) spoils system, which is the sorry mess that civil rights advocacy has become in America since the death of Martin Luther King. What is at stake here, of course, is not rights but entitlements: the set asides, grants, voting district lines, and government (and now private) handouts which serve as payoffs to the racial/ethnic (take-your-pick) grievance-mongers that the demise of the civil rights movement has spawned. Otherwise, who could be against a multiracial census category that, if adopted, would embody the celebrated American mosaic touted by former New York City Mayor David Dinkins and others?

Actually, I would be against it. I say this, not only as a veteran of the once venerable civil rights movement, but as the grandfather of three beautiful granddaughters who would qualify for the box that will not appear on your next national census—and thus will not qualify for the affirmative action perks, the special even-if-you-don't-really-need-them scholarships, and the minority even-if-you-have-to-subcontract-them-to-someone-who-is-actually-qualified-to-do-the-job contracts. Of course, my granddaughters will be able to fill a racial box anyway and qualify for all these even-if-they-don't-deserve-them perks, if they just tick off the category which includes that part of their racial/ethnic (take-your-pick) chromosomes that make the Clinton liberals and other social engineers of the new American apartheid feel good about themselves.

I use the word "apartheid," advisedly, because apartheid in its origins as well as its development was nothing more than an affirmative action program for the Boer minority (oppressed by the English). The term "multiracial," as a government category, immediately brought to my mind a trip I took to South Africa in the last days of the apartheid system, where I encountered the term "colored" or "mixed-race" as an emblem of the extreme to which such affirmative action programs can eventually lead.

The current multiracial census fiasco ought to set off an alarm bell to the nation. We have already become a race-conscious society in a way that would have been unthinkable just a generation ago, when the phrase "without regard to race, color, or creed," was still invoked whenever anyone wanted to sum up "the American Way." Where will the present path lead—down a road to deeper and more bitter racial divisions, ugly struggles over diminishing racial spoils, increasing civil conflict, and eventually a South African future? Or perhaps just further into the realm of the ridiculous and the just plain stupid? I have no idea. But you can check one of the above.

Bilingual Oppression

Cambodians, Laotians, Koreans, Chinese, and Vietnamese come to America and are forced to learn English. And do very well. They score at the highest levels of any ethnic groups on those Eurocentrically-biased standard performance tests, get into the most elite colleges in impressive numbers, and go on to become businessmen, engineers, and computer scientists. And do it all without affirmative action quotas or special language programs. In fact, the affirmative action quotas are largely there to keep their Asian numbers down, so that lower-scoring Mexicans, Latinos, and other government-privileged minorities can get in.

On the other hand, Mexicans and other Latinos come to America and—especially in California—are placed by liberal educators in "bilingual" programs, where they are taught in their native tongues, and where English is a second language. And often not even a language that is spoken at all. The majority of the 330,000 Latino children in California's bilingual education programs are limited by the administrators to one-half hour of English per eight-hour day. The results are an abysmal 6 percent annual rate in moving Latino students from Spanish-taught to English-taught classes, a record-high 50 percent drop-out rate, low test scores for the students who graduate, and low-paying jobs for the community as a whole.

Thank you liberals. The California bilingual program, launched through the efforts of Chicano activists and defended by the Ford-funded Mexican American Legal Defense and Educational Fund, the teachers unions and the "progressive" lobby is the largest such program in the nation. It costs three hundred and twenty million dollars annually.

But now it is under siege. And by the Latino community itself. The rebellion began with a protest boycott of two hundred poverty stricken immigrant parents who reacted when their children were forced into Spanish language classes after they had requested English. They kept their children home and won the support of Republican Mayor Richard Riordan until the school was embarrassed enough to back down and provide them with English instruction.

Enter Ron Unz, right-wing Republican candidate in the last gubernatorial election and Silicon Valley millionaire. Unz has put his money behind a ballot measure for next year's election called the "English for the Children" initiative. Imagine! In 1997, in America, it will take a ballot initiative to give Spanish-speaking immigrants the right to have their children educated in the language of the country in which they have chosen to live, and thus gain the opportunity to succeed!

Bilingualism, like its sister multiculturalism, is really a vast patronage and jobs program for liberal activists and their friends. That is why the year-in and year-out failure of bilingual programs and their youthful inmates, the prospect of opportunity denied to already poor and vulnerable people, has had no impact so far on the liberal conscience. The liberal politicians and organized spokesmen for the Latino community are too busy lining the pockets of their friends and political supporters, to care.

Actually, not all liberals have remained so deaf to the cries of the oppressed. One who long ago had second thoughts is Gloria Matta Tuchman, an award-winning Mexican American educator who has spent twenty years teaching first graders in Santa Ana through the "immersion" method. The idea is obvious and simple. Young children pick up new languages much more easily than adults. Throw them into a class where English is the language, and they will learn. Which is just what they do under Tuchman's tutelage. Fully 99 percent of her first grade pupils move into English classes every year. The success rate should sell itself, but the politically correct Santa Ana school board will have none of it, for the reasons cited above.

Now Tuchman has joined Unz in a coalition that includes Latinos, conservatives, and even leftists in support of the "English for the Children" initiative. One of these is Alice Callaghan, who runs the Las Familias del Pueblo children's center on Skid Row in downtown Los Angeles. It was Callaghan who helped organize the boycott that sparked the new movement. In the most revealing comment of the day, she told reporter Jill Stewart, "This is the first politically incorrect thing I have ever done in my life."

Why is this so politically incorrect? Why does liberalism think that Latinos, blacks, and other designated minorities need endless government-provided crutches to succeed in a country where Cambodian and Vietnamese boat-people do so well without them? In the history of this country, immigrants from literally hundreds of non-English speaking nations have come here, been immersed in an English-speaking culture and climbed the American ladder of success. Why are Latinos such a privileged (and under-privileged) group in the liberal perspective? When are liberals going to treat Latinos and other people who are of different ethnic backgrounds as they would treat themselves? When are they going to set them free?

Black History Lesson

Fifty years ago this spring, Jackie Robinson broke the color bar in baseball. The events that followed provide a lesson for Black History month that many civil rights leaders seem to have forgotten. Following Robinson's historic breakthrough, as everybody knows, other black athletes followed his example and professional basketball and football also became multiracial sports. Over the years there were many who doubted that these gains were possible or that the revolution would continue. The doubters said whites would never accept more than a few black players; that there would always be quotas to limit their number. Whites, they said, would never allow blacks to become managers or quarterbacks or the owners of clubs. They said that if blacks became the majority of the players in professional basketball whites would no longer go to see the games.

But history has shown that the doubters were wrong. Blacks did become managers and quarterbacks, and general managers. Superstars like Isaiah Thomas and Magic Johnson even became owners. So thoroughly did blacks come to dominate sports that were once the exclusive province of whites, that in basketball today almost ninety percent of the starting players are black. When the All-Star game was played this year, it was televised to one hundred and seventy countries worldwide, and nine out of the ten starting players were black multimillionaires, some with contracts totaling fifty, eighty, and even a hundred million dollars. Despite this overwhelming tide of color in the sport, 80 percent of the paying customers were still white.

But the most telling point in the history just summarized is the following neglected fact: This was all accomplished without government intervention and without affirmative action. There were no government policies or official guidelines laid down for owners of athletic teams, no EEOC investigators hovering around stadiums or summoning owners to court. No lawsuits were filed by NAACP lawyers, no consent decrees ordered by federal judges, no heavy government hand compelling owners to redress "past injustice." All that was required to achieve this momentous change in America's race relations was two things: A single business-man with a vision, and a public to support him.

To begin the process towards equality, it was necessary that one man recognize the injustice and have the courage of his conviction. That man was Branch Rickey, the owner of the Brooklyn Dodgers. It was Branch Rickey and Branch Rickey alone who decided to hire Jackie Robinson and make baseball a multiracial sport. To complete the process, however, a second element was indispensable: The goodwill of the white fans. If whites had turned away from the game because of the presence of black players, Branch Rickey's efforts would have failed. But the crowds kept coming. Other owners, needing the best players to transform their clubs into winning teams, and seeing that the fans would accept players of any race, followed Rickey's example. And that was how the face of America's sports industry was changed.

Sports club owners are not the most enlightened segments of the population, and neither perhaps are sports fans themselves. But they have shown over half a century that they are not racists either. Given the choice, they will accept black Americans, recognize their achievements, and even worship them as popular icons and heroes, rewarding them like kings in the process. So tolerant is the real America in 1997, that a black transvestite named Dennis Rodman, with orange and sometimes green hair, and rings through his nose, can earn upwards of twenty to thirty million dollars a year, be sought after for product endorsements, be a Hollywood movie star, and become an idol to millions of white American youngsters. These are facts that need to be remembered at a time when so many "civil rights leaders" dwell only on the negative aspects of our racial present and past.

The corrosive effect of affirmative action policies that insist on government-ordered racial preferences is to make America forget this history, and to convince black Americans that without government coercion, and court decrees, they cannot get the justice they deserve. It is to convince them that whites are hopelessly racist and that current black success depends on government agencies forcing whites to be fair. This is a perverse argument and I leave it to armchair psychologists to figure out why it is so persuasive. After all, the government is also dominated by the white majority. Why should whites in government be able to deliver the justice that whites elsewhere deny? How did whites create affirmative action policies in the first place if their intentions were, as Jesse Jackson is forever complaining, to "lock" blacks out?

Jackie Robinson was able to break the color bar and enter the major leagues because he was better than most of the players at the time. The injustice of his exclusion was obvious first to one man. But once Robinson had a chance to show what he could do, it was obvious to all. Americans are by and large a fair-minded people. As we commemorate Black History Month, it's time for us all to acknowledge this fact.

Martin's Children

D uring the darkest days of the Cold War, the Italian writer Ignazio Silone predicted that the final struggle of the great conflict would be between the Communists and the ex-Communists. And so it seems among civil rights activists in the war over affirmative action.

Jesse Jackson and the opponents of Proposition 209, which outlaws government race preferences, claim for themselves the mantle of the civil rights movement. Led by Jackson, opponents of 209 even staged a protest march in San Francisco on the anniversary of Martin Luther King's famous Washington moment to make the point. But the architects of Proposition 209, and its principal spokesmen, are also veterans of King's movement. It is no accident (as radicals like to say) that Proposition 209 is called "The California Civil Rights Initiative," or that its text is carefully constructed to conform to the letter and spirit of the landmark Civil Rights Acts of 1964 and1965.

Obviously it is not the goal of ending racism that divides the former activists. It is, rather, conflicting memories of the past and differing strategies for the future. How much racial progress has been made since the federal government embraced the civil rights agenda? What is the best way to overcome the racial inequalities that persist?

For the anti-209 marchers, the answer is simple: Racism has not changed its substance, only its form. In this view, whatever gains blacks have made have been forced upon a recalcitrant white populace. A race neutral government would allow historic prejudice to reassert itself and do its malevolent work. The inequalities themselves, without remedial effort, would create new injustice. The cure, therefore, must be continued government intervention. To eliminate affirmative action policies, both Jesse Jackson and President Clinton have warned, is to invite the "re-segregation" of American life.

Into this dispute comes a massive new scholarly book by two civil rights veterans. Stephan and Abigail Thernstrom's *America In Black and White* reconstructs the history of racial progress and conflict in the postwar era, and examines the impact of affirmative action solutions. For the perspective advanced by Clinton and Jackson, they cite Atlanta's black mayor, who in 1996 claimed that every black person in America "has benefitted from affirmative action. There's not been anybody who's gotten a job on their own, no one who's prospered as a businessman or businesswoman on their own . . . ."

Yet consider these unruly facts presented in the Thernstroms' book:

In 1940, 87 percent of American blacks lived in poverty. By 1960—five years before the civil rights acts and ten years before the first affirmative action policies—the figure was down to 47 percent. This twenty year drop was an even greater and more rapid decline in black poverty than took place over the next thirty-five years of affirmative action policies and anti-poverty programs, a period which saw the black poverty rate come down to 26 percent as of 1995.

In 1940, only 5 percent of black men and 6.4 percent of black women had middle class occupations. By 1970, the figures were 22 percent for black men (a nearly four-fold increase) and 36 percent for black women (a nearly five-fold increase)—larger again than the increase that took place in the twenty years after affirmative action was put in place (roughly 1970) when the figures reached 32 percent and 59 percent.

The cause of black poverty, as the Thernstroms show, has little to do with race and, therefore, its solution will not be affected by affirmative action set-asides. Currently, for example, 85 percent of all poor black children live in fatherless families. The poverty rate for black children without fathers is nearly five times that for black children with two parents. A far more effective anti-poverty program than current government handouts would be to promote black marriages.

Even in higher education, affirmative action has not been the indispensable as its advocates imply. The rate of gain for blacks in college enrollments was greater between 1960 and 1970 (when enrollments for blacks increased from 4 percent to 7 percent of the total college population), before affirmative action policies were instituted, than it was in the decades after, when it went from 7 percent to 9.9 percent between 1970 and 1980, and from 9.9 percent to 10.7 percent between 1980 and 1994.

Of course, before affirmative action many of these students were attending all black colleges in the South. The really significant gain was in greater "diversity." The proportion of black students enrolled in predominantly white schools quadrupled between 1960 and 1980. This made white liberals and—to be fair—whites generally, feel good. But was it as good for the black students who were enrolled, particularly those who were accepted to schools because of affirmative action double standards?

In 1965—before these policies were put in place—blacks were only about half as likely to actually graduate college as whites. In 1995—after affirmative action took effect—the figure was exactly the same. Although almost half of African Americans in the twenty-to-twenty-five age bracket had been enrolled in college (as of 1995) barely one in seven of them held a bachelor's degree.

In the economic sphere, affirmative action policies had the net effect not of employing greater numbers of blacks or raising their living standards, but of shifting black employment from small businesses to large corporations and to government agencies. In higher education, the net effect of affirmative action has been even more perverse. In a system organized as a hierarchy of merit, a good student who can get A's at San Francisco State might flunk out at Harvard, In 1995, there were only one thousand seven hundred and sixty-four black students nationwide who scored as high as six hundred on the verbal SATs (the math scores were even worse). But, under affirmative action guidelines, all of those students were recruited to Berkeley, Harvard and similar elite schools where the average white student (not to mention the average Asian) normally had scores at least one hundred points (and more likely two hundred) higher.

In short, at every level of the university system, the net effect of affirmative action has been to place African Americans in college programs that exceed their qualifications. This is the unspoken nightmare of affirmative action for the very minorities for whom it was designed. At Berkeley, the gap in SAT scores between blacks and whites is nearly three hundred points. Predictably, blacks drop out of Berkeley at nearly three times the rate of whites. As the Thernstroms ruefully observe, in the age of affirmative action the college that comes closest to racial equality in actually graduating its students is Ole Miss, once the last bastion of segregation in the South. Although integrated now, Ole Miss is resistant to the new racial duplicity in admissions standards. The result is that 49 percent of all whites who enter Ole Miss as freshmen graduate, and so do 48 percent of all blacks.

On the basis of what actually has happened over the last five decades, it is clear that affirmative action is 1) unnecessary to racial progress; 2) actively destructive to its supposed beneficiaries; and 3) useless in making up the continuing income and education gaps. Its real effect is to create black failure and additional grievance, and to stir the resentment of other groups (not only whites but Asians) who see themselves displaced, on the basis of race, from their hard won places of merit.

Yet another veteran of the civil rights movement, Jim Sleeper, has just weighed in with a book specifically addressed to this toxic effect of liberal good intentions. In *Liberal Racism* he writes "Liberalism no longer curbs discrimination. It invites it. It does not expose racism; it recapitulates and, sometimes, reinvents it."

Thus does the cold war between the children of Martin Luther King beget ironies without end.

The President's Challenge

ill Clinton's much-awaited statement on race has come and gone, and—as usual with this president—no one on either side of the argument is convinced that anything was said at all. But perhaps this does reflect something about the general public consciousness at this point in time—a reflection of the nation's inability to speak clearly, unambiguously and directly about the issue of race. The President's words perfectly crystallize this problem.

The President chose a University of California campus in San Diego as the site for his pronouncement in order to focus attention on California's ban on racial preferences and on the drop in enrollment rates as a result of that ban. According to University officials, African-American admissions to U.C.'s Boalt law school—one of the most prestigious in the nation—dropped by 85 percent because of the new policy.

One lesson of this result that the President pointedly did not discuss was the way in which it completely undermined the arguments of the defenders of the affirmative action policies that are now illegal. In the arguments over the California Civil Rights Initiative, its opponents had argued that race was only one of many factors and an insignificant one at best in awarding affirmative action places at the university. Now it is clear to all that affirmative action is indeed a system of racial preferences and racial discrimination, and nothing more.

The President calls for a conversation about race, but what he really wants is a conversation about racism, and about white racism at that. His response to California's rejection of racial preferences: "We must not re-segregate higher education"—as though the re-segregation of higher education were not already an accomplished fact; as though black separatists (and their liberal allies) were not the leaders of the re-segregation movement—the separate black dorms and black graduations, the African-American studies programs and special orientations for incoming black freshmen, the expensive invitations to black racists like Khalid Muhammad, Louis Farrakhan, Kwame Ture, Professor Griff, Sister Souljah, Leonard Jeffries, Tony Martin, Frances Welsing etc., etc. to speak before black student unions and "Pan African" student associations about the evils of whiteness.

Lacking any interest in addressing the real problems of racial division in America, the President chose instead to offer a challenge to those of us who remain faithful to the vision of the civil rights movement and still reject government discrimination, whoever is proposing it and whatever the justification: "To those who oppose affirmative action," the President said, "I ask you to come up with an alternative. I would embrace it if I could find a better way."

There is such an alternative, Mr. President, it is called *study.* Study hard. If you want to get into an elite law school, that's the way to do it. Is there anybody who seriously believes that admissions officials at America's liberal universities are actual racists, determined to keep black applicants out? Nobody actually claims this, because the truth is that universities are desperate to get black applicants in. That is why the affirmative action crowd is not clamoring for new admissions officers, but new (and lower) standards instead.

The alternative to rigging the standards is, of course, to teach one's children the value of an education in the first place. It is to stick around after conception to help one's child enter a difficult and demanding world. It is to give up the blame game and look at one's own responsibility for where one is. It is to tell one's children that getting educated is not—as many in the black community will say—"thinking white." It's thinking. Period.

How can it be helpful to African Americans to suggest, as liberals do, that they are failing to meet academic standards because white racists want to keep them out? This is a lie and everybody knows it. African Americans are failing because they are not prepared by their families and their culture to succeed. If race or poverty were the issue, the University of California would not be excluding Vietnamese and Cambodian children (who do meet the standards) in order to make room for African American and Hispanic children (who do not).

It's time to stop pandering to minority racists and to stop patronizing minorities in general. It's time for a president of the United States to stand up and be proud of the fact that in America minorities are no longer barred because of race from America's best universities, or indeed from any American university. Racial hand-wringing by liberal whites does not help the disadvantaged. On the contrary, it is an obstacle to their progress. It contributes to what is now a massive denial of the problems that minority communities have created for themselves. And by contributing to the delusion that it is hostile Others who have been successful in life, who control their destinies, this liberal myth takes away from minorities the real power they have to change their fate.

An Academic Lynching

L ino Graglia is a 67-year old Sicilian who was an attorney in the Eisenhower Justice Department and has been teaching Constitutional Law at the University of Texas in Austin for thirty-three years. A Catholic conservative, stiff-necked and intellectually eccentric (it goes with the territory), Graglia is a distinguished legal scholar and a textualist when it comes to constitutional doctrine. If representatives of the sovereign people choose to enact a law that is not contradicted by the actual text, the law is constitutional. But this view is not what has made him the center of a public burning.

And a burning it is. In the past week, the president of his university, the chancellor and fifty-one of his law school colleagues have denounced him. State legislators, including the chairman of the Hispanic Caucus, have described him as a Ku Klux Klanner, a racist, and "academic riff-raff," and have called for his immediate dismissal. The *Houston Chronicle* has editorially condemned him as an "embarrassment" to the university and the state. The NAACP and three student groups have charged him with "racial harassment," and Jesse Jackson—friend of Al Sharpton and Louis Farrakhan—has condemned him before five thousand cheering campus demonstrators for "racist, fascist, offensive speech," while calling on students to boycott his classes and "turn him into a moral and social pariah." Other speakers were even less restrained and demanded that the university fire him.

The anti-Graglia frenzy has been so strong that out of a faculty of more than a thousand professors only two have been willing to come forward to defend the character of a man who has taught for thirty-three years among them without any significant complaint against him, and whose Dean, after reviewing his personal file, issued a public statement saying that there were no grounds for disciplinary action and that "the record does not justify a charge that he discriminates against his students and others on the basis of race or ethnicity." Indeed, as the *Chronicle* reported, "no one has offered any evidence that Graglia treats minority and white students differently."

Graglia's crime? Telling an uncomfortable truth, and telling it a little off-key. Twenty years ago Graglia wrote a book called *Disaster by Decree: The Supreme Court Decisions on Race and the Schools*. He is accustomed to describing affirmative action programs as a "fungus" and a "fraud," but was unprepared for the hysteria of the present outbreak, particularly since the remarks that provoked the reaction were tepid by comparison to what he had intended. His real offense, it seemed, was talking to the press.

Graglia had been invited to give a speech to the first meeting of the "Students for Equal Opportunity," whose faculty advisor he was. The topic of his remarks was the *Hopwood* case, which recently ended affirmative action at the University of Texas Law School. In his remarks, Graglia said "the only reason we have racial preferences, of course, is the fact that blacks and Mexican-Americans are not academically competitive with whites and Asians. Racial preferences are simply an attempt to conceal or wish away this unwelcome fact."

In the press report, however, this statement became: "Blacks and Mexican Americans can't compete academically with whites." Both statements are factual, but in the second there is a nuance which could be taken to imply that the minorities in question (notice how the Asians drop from view when the press takes charge) can't by nature compete academically with whites.

Alert to this nuance (indeed probably salivating at it) the same reporter asked Graglia what he thought caused the gap in performance on standardized tests. Graglia answered that he didn't know. The reporter pressed on. Did Graglia think the cause was "genetic or cultural?" Graglia said he thought it was cultural, and suggested that perhaps less academically successful groups put less emphasis on academic achievement and did not necessarily consider academic failure "a disaster." Later, Graglia explained how in his own Sicilian household as a child academic achievement was given less emphasis than among many Jewish households he knew.

In the press account this speculation came out as a presumptive and defining declaration: "'It is the result primarily of cultural effects. Various studies seem to show that blacks and Mexican Americans spend much less time in school,' he said. 'They have a culture that seems not to encourage achievement. Failure is not looked upon with disgrace.'"

These are the comments that have made a distinguished professor of law a pariah in his own community and an object of public contempt. Yet this surely should surprise no one. The atmosphere of progressive intimidation, which is even thicker on college campuses today than anti-Communist paranoia was in the McCarthy era, has a purpose which is well understood. It is to suppress the dirty secret of affirmative action. The preferential race policies, which thanks to *Hopwood* and other decisions are now in their death throes, are built on the very premise for which Graglia is under attack: Blacks, Hispanics, and other minorities designated for affirmative action preferences cannot compete intellectually on standardized tests. Asians, of course, can (and are therefore not designated for affirmative action favors). The lynching of Lino Graglia is an effort to suppress this discomforting truth.

Ironically, this was the text of Graglia's actual remarks before the Students for Equal Opportunity, which have now been securely buried under an Everest of invective:

> Racial preferences are the root cause of virtually all the major problems plaguing American campuses today. They result in a student body with two groups, identifiable by race, who inhabit different academic ballparks. An inability to compete successfully in the game being played necessarily results in demands that the game be changed. This is the way

demands for black and Hispanic studies, 'multiculturalism,' racial diversity, and rigged standards are born. Little is more humiliating to the racially preferred than open discussion of the conditions of their admission.
Concealment and deception are always essential elements of racial pref-
erence programs—and thus is born insistence on political correctness
and the need [to suppress] 'hate speech.'

Which, on liberal American campuses, has become mainly another name for
challenges to the status quo.

Choke Your Coach, Become a Cause

T ry this exercise: Imagine that a white player for the National Basketball
Association had first tried to strangle his black coach and then threatened
to kill him in front of the whole team, Latrell Sprewell of the Golden
State Warriors just did. Suppose that this white player had previously threatened a
team-mate with a gun and a two-by-four, just like Sprewell. Suppose the league,
responding to such unprofessional, even criminal conduct, suspended the white
player for a year and that his team terminated his contract. How many public figures do you think would step forward to defend the culprit? How many mayors of
major cities would speak out in his behalf, as Willie Brown and two other black
mayors did in behalf of Sprewell, even suggesting that "maybe the coach deserved
to be choked"? How many white players would stand behind the culprit at his press
conference to show support the way Sprewell's black teammates did for him? How
many famous white lawyers would "join his team" and claim, as Johnnie Cochran
did, that there had been a "rush to judgment" and a "disparity in treatment," imply-
ing that race was the issue and the player was being punished only because his victim was black?

Here's another exercise: Imagine that a white football star had a history of brutality towards his black wife, and then one day the wife was found savagely murdered. Suppose he attempted to flee when the police named him a suspect in the
murder. Suppose his blood was found all over the crime scene, and the blood of his
dead wife on his clothes, his car and at his home. Suppose that a 911 recording of
her screams that he was going to murder her was played to the court and to the
whole country. What are the chances that a white jury would have acquitted him in
less than an hour? Or that whites all over the country would publicly cheer such a
racially malicious verdict, rather than hang their heads in collective shame?

And here's another: Imagine that Rodney King had been white. Picture a convicted white felon, a wife-beater and parole violator, fleeing the law at one hundred miles an hour, sexually taunting a female police officer, throwing policemen from his back and otherwise physically resisting arrest. Would anyone have paid the slightest attention if the police had given him some extra whacks? Would the president of the United States have called for the arresting officers to be tried and then tried twice, until they were sent to jail? Would the white felon have been given three million dollars in compensation by a contrite City Hall and made a poster-boy for police brutality and racial injustice by the nation as a whole?

These exercises show what is missing from the current dialogue on race: A candid discussion of the way white America has been overreacting to the shame of its receding racial past, and then of the way the race card has become such an all-purpose excuse for black America that many prominent black figures don't seem to be able to leave home without it. Are blacks failing to keep up educationally with Asians and whites? It must be "institutional racism" that is to blame. Are blacks committing crimes out of all proportion to their representation in the population? It must be a racist criminal justice system that is responsible. Are a few high paid black thugs threatening to ruin a sport that blacks have come to dominate? It's just whites rushing to judgment and calling for disparate punishments because the perpetrators are black.

The problem with the current national dialogue on race is that it has been framed by people for whom there is only one acceptable conclusion: Blacks are victims; whites are to blame. That is why the chairman of the President's commission on race excluded the chief critic of affirmative action from the discussion (even though he also happens to be black). Racial payback for blacks is what the argument for affirmative action has become. To oppose this "solution" is to blame the victim.

This all may have been a plausible scenario thirty-odd years ago, when segregation was alive and well in the American South. But in the America of the '90s, where black multimillionaires like Latrell Sprewell constitute 80 percent of the NBA players, and whites make up 80 percent of the paying customers, where black millionaire mayors like Willie Brown call the shots in major cities, where black millionaire lawyers like Johnnie Cochran are national celebrities and command national audiences, this is just plain dumb.

And the rest of America knows it is. In fact, the negative reaction to the Sprewell incident by liberal sportswriters and commentators shows that the rest of America may at last be ready to say it out loud. Americans have had it up to the ears with the blame-games of blacks and the self-flagellating responses of whites. This is in no small part because they have come to see that such attitudes only make things worse. This is not equality. It's the master-slave relationship reversed.

The Sprewell affair shows that we are approaching the end of an era, which is the best news about race yet. White America has changed. All blacks no longer "look alike." Even ordinary Americans—sports fans, for instance—no longer look at blacks as the anonymous Other—the inscrutable menace or the universal victim. White America can tell the difference between a Latrell Sprewell and a Michael Jordan, between a Christopher Darden and a Johnnie Cochran, a Ward Connerly and a Willie Brown. And there's hope in that.

Progressive Education

Of all the misnomers of our political vocabulary, "progressive" is probably the most abusive and certainly the most abused. "Progressive" is the accepted term for the political left today, just as it was fifty years ago, when it was used as a self-description by Communists and fellow-travelers who sought its protective cover even as they supported the most oppressive regimes in human history. In the later years of the Cold War, it was the term of choice for liberals as well, who thought that the Soviet system was "converging" with Reagan's America, just before the Communist fall.

One of the more interesting characteristics of progressives is the way they seem to learn nothing from their experience, confounding the very idea of progress as a process of escaping from the myths of the past and acquiring knowledge. Today, self-styled "progressives" can be found supporting economic redistribution and state-sponsored racial discrimination, or memorializing the death anniversaries of totalitarian legends like Che Guevara, just as though the history of the last half-century had never taken place. And progressives can still be counted on to lend their support to the discredited domestic legends of Sixties "revolutions," most notably the Black Panther vanguard.

In Oakland, recently, something calling itself the Dr. Huey P. Newton Foundation launched a "Legacy Tour" of "historic" Black Panther sites as a step towards making the Panther stronghold into a local monument like Lexington and Valley Forge. On a glistening October day, three busloads of former Panthers and Panther supporters, along with Oakland city officials, began the tour with visits to the Oakland homes of Huey Newton, Bobby Seale, and Panther "Field Marshal" David Hilliard. Hilliard, who was their guide for the day, once spent a year in jail for threatening to kill President Nixon in front of one hundred thousand anti-war protesters in Golden Gate Park. Now Hilliard describes himself as a recovering drug addict and alcoholic, and executive director of the Dr. Huey P. Newton Foundation. Other sites included various Panther headquarters; the street corner where Huey Newton shot an Oakland police officer in an incident that launched the "Free Huey" movement and made the Panthers a national cause; the shootout scene where a Panther named Bobby Hutton was killed after a Party hit squad attacked San Francisco police in an attempt to "avenge" the assassination of Martin Luther King; and the sidewalk where Huey Newton met his long-deserved end at the hands of a crack cocaine dealer he had burned.

Not included in the Legacy Tour were the sites where Huey Newton killed an eighteen-year-old black prostitute, raped a black mother of three, and shotgunned the doorman of an "after hours" club which had refused to cooperate in a Panther shakedown. Also missing were stops at the sites where Party members were "mud-holed," whipped with cat-o-nine tails, or beaten with chains by Newton's goon squad for infractions of Party discipline. (One editor of the Party paper, by her own account, was bullwhipped for not meeting an editorial deadline.) Missing also was a visit to the house where Panthers tortured former *Ramparts* employee Betty Van Patter, before smashing her head with a pipe and throwing her body into San Francisco Bay.

Tour guide Hilliard instead stressed the Panthers' "idealism" and explained how "the point to be made is that when you fall below history as happened with women and slaves, you're really nothing. So the point we're trying to make here is to not be written out of history but to be a part of history." The enthusiastic audience for these pieties included the sitting Mayor of Oakland, members of the Oakland City Council, the Oakland Board of Education (the same that adopted "ebonics" as an "official language"), and former California Governor Jerry Brown, now running for mayor with David Hillard as his chief of staff.

A straight-faced account of the "Tour of Panther Sites" appeared in the *San Francisco Chronicle* complete with accompanying tour map. It began: "The Black Panther Party for Self-Defense was about politics, as its name implies, not about destruction." None of the missing pieces of Panther history were alluded to in the *San Francisco Chronicle* account (the *Chronicle* has been a long-time booster of this urban gang), nor in similar credulous reports on National Public Radio and in he *New York Times*.

This was more than a case of collective amnesia. After all, America is not a progressive police state as the Soviet Union once was, where you can simply erase the historical record. It's not as if the sordid history of Panthers, a homicidal street gang with political pretensions, is not widely known. But as Michael Kelly recently observed in the *New Republic*, the journalistic ranks are filled with veterans of the counterculture who consider themselves progressive and who supported the revolutions of that time. Their duplicity is reinforced by younger black reporters, guided by the principle of not speaking ill of the "brothers" and lending ammunition to whitey's fears. These guardians of the public truth have taken it upon themselves to protect the Panther myth and, more importantly, the progressive cause the myth supports. The result is a national media which acts to "institutionalize the myth of the Panthers" and of the "progressive" Sixties.

This mentality was on full display in the national coverage of Black Panther Geronimo Pratt's release from prison on a technicality last July. Although Pratt had been convicted of an unusually cold-blooded murder, not a single reporter interviewed prosecutors in the case, let alone Pratt's chief accuser, a former Black Panther named Julius Butler, in an effort to gain a reasonably balanced view. Nor did a single reporter bother to look at the court records in the case, which prove beyond the shadow of a doubt that Pratt did murder elementary school teacher Caroline Olsen on a Santa Monica tennis court twenty-nine years ago. Instead the press repeated Johnnie Cochran's unchallenged fantasies of an FBI-LAPD conspiracy to frame Pratt, despite the fact that the evidence originally presented at trial shows that there could not have been such a conspiracy. While ignoring Pratt's prosecutors, the press amplified the claims of his supporters and fans, who view him as an "American Nelson Mandela" and a new progressive hero. After his release, journalists followed Pratt deferentially on his own tour of college campuses and dutifully reported the book and film deals he was negotiating which will undoubtedly further lionize his criminal life.

And so history repeats itself, as Hegel once said, the first time as tragedy, the second as farce. Today's progressives are like nothing so much as the Bourbons, of whom it was once said, "They learn nothing and forget nothing."

Geronimo Pratt

L os Angeles District Attorney Gil Garcetti is to be applauded for his decision to try to send convicted murderer and former Black Panther Geronimo Pratt back to jail. Garcetti has just filed a two hundred-page appeal of the judicial ruling that freed Pratt after Johnnie Cochran and his legal defense team argued that their client was the target of a conspiracy by FBI-Cointelpro operatives, the LAPD, and the District Attorney's office to frame the Black Panther leader. At the time, the *Los Angeles Times* and other media reporting the case gave Cochran and Pratt such a free ride, that citizens unfamiliar with the facts will find it hard to grasp the merits of Garcetti's decision. But as Garcetti himself has said: "Nothing that has been learned about this case in the twenty-five years since it was tried, or in the twenty-nine years since Caroline Olsen was murdered, warrants a new trial."

That Geronimo Pratt was the gunman who fired the fatal shots into the prone figure of elementary school teacher Caroline Olsen on that Santa Monica tennis court in December 1968 is as certain as any such claim can be. Pratt was identified by eyewitnesses; his red GTO convertible with distinctive North Carolina plates was placed at the scene of the crime; and his signature .45 caliber hand gun was shown to be the murder weapon. Worse still, he boasted of his crime to Julius Butler, the man whose reputation Cochran and a pliant media successfully destroyed in order to get Pratt released.

Not surprisingly, Cochran's tactics in freeing Pratt directly paralleled those he made famous in getting O.J. Simpson acquitted: Paint law enforcement as a conspiracy of racists and trust white guilt and black resentment to do the rest. There was no Mark Fuhrman in the Pratt case, so Julius Butler, once a Panther himself and subsequently a board member of the AME Church, a lawyer, and a respected member of the African-American community of Los Angeles, was picked to be the fall guy.

Butler had been the chief witness for the prosecution. Cochran's successful appeal was based on the claim that Butler was a police "informant" and that the prosecution had concealed from the original jury Butler's contacts with law enforcement, which Cochran manipulated into conspiratorial intent. If the original trial jury had been informed of these contacts, Cochran argued, the verdict might have been different.

But the facts say otherwise. For a trail of evidence exists in this case that systematically refutes any hypothesis of a frame-up.

Caroline Olsen was murdered on December 18, 1968. Almost nine months later, on August 10, 1969, a terrified Julius Butler met with black LAPD officer Sergeant Duwayne Rice and delivered into Rice's safe-keeping a sealed envelope. Butler had been assigned by the Panthers to be their official liaison with the police, and knew Rice in that capacity. The envelope he gave to Rice contained a letter detailing death threats that Pratt and his lieutenants had made against Butler.

The Panthers had been a Watts street gang called the Slausons, and were led by former Slauson gang leader Alprentice "Bunchy" Carter. When Carter and another Panther named John Huggins were killed by members of Ron Karenga's rival political gang ("US"), in a shooting at UCLA in January 1969, Pratt became head of the Party. His first order of business was ferreting out suspected "US" agents. One of his targets was Julius Butler.

In the sealed letter Butler delivered to Sergeant Rice, he sought to establish that the death threats Pratt was directing at him should be taken seriously. He said that Pratt had "bragged" to him about "acts of murder" he had committed—including "the killing of a white school teacher and the wounding of her husband on a tennis court in the city of Santa Monica sometime during the year of 1968." Butler asked Sergeant Rice to keep the envelope as "insurance" for him, and not to open it until after his death. That envelope remained sealed for fourteen more months until October 1970—a fact completely at odds with any "frame-up" theory. The opening of Julius Butler's sealed letter with these charges led directly to the arraignment of Geronimo Pratt in December 1970.

If there had indeed been a law enforcement conspiracy against Pratt, in which Butler was involved, why did it take so long for law enforcement to pry the information from Butler and Rice? All the evidence Cochran has marshaled of Butler's contacts with law enforcement to establish his case—regardless of how they are interpreted—took place after the sealed note identifying his client as the killer was delivered into the hands of Sergeant Rice. None of Cochran's claims about Butler being a police "informant" affect the incriminating contents of the envelope one iota.

The FBI had observed Butler handing over the envelope to Rice on August 10, 1969. Three days later, on August 13, they approached Butler and began what was to be a fourteen-month campaign of pressures and threats against him to force him to hand over the envelope. (These are among the contacts that Cochran converts into the conclusion that Butler was a police "informant.") The FBI and the LAPD also threatened Sergeant Rice with prosecution for his refusal to turn over the envelope. And for fourteen months he also refused. How could Butler and Rice be part of an FBI-police conspiracy to "get" Geronimo Pratt and at the same time refuse to turn over the crucial incriminating evidence against Pratt? This is a question that Johnnie Cochran has not answered and that the judge whom he persuaded to release Pratt did not even bother to consider.

Even the sequence of events which led to the opening of the envelope in October 1970—twenty-two months after the murder—dramatically refutes Cochran's conspiratorial imputations. During these fourteen months, Sergeant Rice knocked down a white police officer and became the subject of an Internal Affairs investigation by the LAPD. The investigators came to suspect that Rice was "subversive" and possibly sympathetic to the Panthers because of his association with Butler (even though Butler was no longer a Panther) and because of his refusal to hand over the envelope. The Internal Affairs investigators of the LAPD threatened Rice with prosecution for withholding the envelope (he had by then given it into the safe-keeping of a black LAPD captain). It was then, threatened with prosecution, that Rice appealed to Butler to let him give up the document.

Far from being the instrument of a Cointelpro and/or police conspiracy, the facts show that Julius Butler was a man caught between two warring forces, neither of which did he wish to collaborate with. The inescapable, undeniable conclusion is that no matter how Johnnie Cochran twists the words "informant" and "conspiracy" to make them apply to Julius Butler, the crucial evidence that incriminates his client was delivered before any contacts took place, and is utterly insulated from them. There, in writing, in an envelope sealed from law enforcement for fourteen months after it was written and withheld in the face of intense law enforcement efforts to obtain it, are the words that damn Geronimo Pratt as guilty of the cold-blooded murder with which he is charged.

Black Racism: The Last Taboo

Just after midnight on the day following black supremacist Louis Farrakhan's "Million Man March," two white men, returning from a reunion, were stopped by black police officers in a black Chicago suburb where they had strayed on the way home. The police officers took one of the two white men—the driver of the vehicle—into custody as a deadbeat dad, and impounded his car. They left his passenger, thirty-two-year-old Richard Will, to walk home. Fifteen minutes later, Will was found near death on the ghetto street. He had been beaten and set on fire by two black thugs and died a few hours later. Later, one of the residents of the neighborhood he was killed in blamed the victim: "What was he doing here? What was a white man doing walking down the street?"

You probably did not read this story in your local press. Not a single newspaper reported the story for ten days, until it was broken by Chicago columnist Mike Royko, who asked whether there would be such disinterest in the story if the victim was black and the lynchers white. It took the *New York Times* another week before the story appeared in its pages on November 5, buried on page eight, and with a headline that did not mention the racial dimension of the case. The *Los Angeles Times* didn't report the story until November 27, and then only on page twenty-seven of its little-read Saturday edition. Its headline—"Death of Man Left by Police in Crime-Ridden Area Probed"—also failed to note that race was involved.

The same week the *Los Angeles Times* story appeared there was another racial murder, even more horrible. An estranged black father and his new girlfriend, also black, killed the two white children of his former lover while sparing the black son they had together. The pair then cut open the pregnant mother's womb to rescue the black infant before killing the mother. The press did not ignore this gruesome incident but failed to make anything of its racial dimension. Imagine the public outcry and editorial hand-wringing if the two murdered children and the murdered mother had been black, and the children spared had been white.

These silences are not unique. In January 1991, Mark Belmore, a white student at Northeastern University in Boston, was murdered by Robert Herbert, who told police that he and three other blacks had agreed to kill the first white person they saw. The story was strictly local news.

In February 1991, a black man named Christopher D. Peterson was arrested in Indiana for killing seven whites with a shotgun. Explaining his crime to police, he said he had "a deep-rooted hatred for white people." The incident was hardly noticed.

In 1991-1992, a trial was held in Florida for members of the "Yahweh" cult. Like Louis Farrakhan, the leader of the cult, Hulon Mitchell, taught his followers that white people were devils. To be initiated into the cult, new members had to kill a white person and cut off an ear as proof of the kill. At the time of the trial, seven persons were known to have been killed. Like the burning of Richard Will in Chicago, the trial of the Yahweh cult leaders went largely unnoticed.

The same may be said of the lynching of Yankel Rosenbaum by a black mob in Crown Heights which chanted "Kill the Jew!" as Rosenbaum was stabbed to death by a black man. The killer confessed to the crime but was then acquitted by an all-black and Puerto Rican jury, who gave a party for the defendant when the trial was over.

Silence—as anti-AIDS activists are quick to point out—sometimes does equal death. Is it an accident that the group whose demonization is most acceptable to our intellectual elites—whites and white males—has become such a target of racial injustice? According to the Uniform Crime Reports of the U. S. Department of Justice for 1994, hate crimes against whites actually exceeded the number of hate crimes against homosexuals, Jews, native Americans, Asian and Pacific Islanders, and Hispanics.

Sixty percent of black Americans, according to a CNN/*Time* poll believe that Louis Farrakhan "speaks the truth." Is it any wonder that in 1994 fifty percent of all racially motivated murders were committed by blacks? (This statistic was reported by the liberal Southern Poverty Law Center.) Or that, according to U.S. crime statistics, the probability of a black offender selecting a white victim is higher than fifty percent? (The probability of a white offender selecting a black victim, according to the same statistics, is only three percent.)

Race hatred is a poison no matter who dishes it out. It's time to put an end to the taboo that protects race-haters if they're black, or that invokes a double-standard by excusing crimes committed against whites as "payback" for "injustices" committed in another time and place.

Gabriel Rotello

Andrew Sullivan

Michelangelo Signorile

Sexual Farragoes

Gay Marriage

As a heterosexual man who is persuaded that most gays are homosexual by nature rather than choice, who holds, therefore, that gays should be accorded the same rights, respect, and moral approbation as everyone else—I nonetheless also believe that the campaign for same-sex "marriage" is misguided, socially destructive, and designed to fail.

The campaign was launched through a favorable court decision in Hawaii and is based on the same elitist principles that have already created powerful backlashes on issues like abortion and prayer in the schools. It is a case of the gay community seeking to force an issue that is radical, deeply personal, and profoundly divisive through the most arbitrary and undemocratic avenue of government available: the liberal courts. Knowing that today they would lose this battle in the legislative arena, which is where the majority gets to have its say, gays decided to use the judiciary to ram through what would be a revolutionary change to an institution that is not only thousands of years old but is generally regarded as the cornerstone of civil society. Under this strategy, a case decided by a court in Hawaii would automatically become law throughout the entire United States including not only other liberal enclaves like Minnesota and Massachusetts but conservative strongholds like Utah, Wyoming, and the Bible Belt South.

What could gay activists have been thinking other than to provoke a gigantic slap in the face? They got the slap they were asking for when their slippery friend in the White House signed the "defense of marriage" bill terminating this phase of their plan.

But what about the merits of the case itself? Andrew Sullivan is a gay conservative, a former editor of the *New Republic*, and the author of *Virtually Normal*, the most intelligent book yet written on the issue. In *Virtually Normal*, Sullivan has made the most incisive case for the institution of gay marriage yet. He has done so again in the preface to his newly published reader *Same-Sex Marriage: Pro and Con*. Sullivan makes a special appeal to his fellow conservatives to endorse gay marriage and thereby to strengthen in the gay community the values of commitment and family it regards as the cornerstone of civilized life in their own.

While I sympathize strongly with this impulse and these ideas, and have great regard for the intellect behind them, I am not persuaded by the case that Andrew and his allies have made.

Or, I should say, partially unpersuaded. I think most Americans would like to see gays enjoy some of the partnership rights that go with marriage, like visitation rights for loved ones in hospitals, to take the one most frequently sited. I think many conservative Americans would agree with Andrew that society has an interest in promoting stability in gay relationships and the kind of restraint of the sexual urge that would promote monogamy in gay households, particularly in the age of AIDS.

But these benefits could be accomplished by something other than marriage. The legal community has a term for it: "domestic partnership" or "registered partnership," a status that would grant state recognition of committed gay relationships but would stop short of transferring all the entitlements associated with marriage in one unreflective act.

And this is and should be a primary concern for the community at large. Marriage is an institution that, as Judge Richard Posner puts it in his contribution to Sullivan's reader, "is a status rich in entitlements." These include not only entitlements with respect to the two parties, but to the children who may issue from the union. The entitlements were designed over hundreds of years with heterosexual and child-rearing couples in mind. To deconstruct this institution overnight would have far-reaching consequences, many of them highly destructive, to the formation and health of a social institution critical for producing the next generation—an institution (need it be emphasized?) that is already in crisis.

What is it that gay people want, that would not be provided by a legal status like "domestic partnership," to make them push so reckless an agenda and invite yet another rejection? Andrew Sullivan provides a clue to the answer: "Granting homosexuals entrance into this institution [of marriage] is tantatamount to complete acceptance of homosexuality by American society. No other measure would signal approval in such a stark and unambiguous way. And many heterosexual Americans are not yet ready to go that far . . . . They are prepared to tolerate, yes, even, in some ways, approve. But they are not yet ready to say that their heterosexual relationships are equivalent to homosexual ones."

This is the crux of the issue. The reality, however, is that heterosexual relationships are not "equivalent" to homosexual ones, anymore than men are equivalent to women. What gays seem to desire at bottom in these self-defeating gestures is that they be regarded as "normal" by the majority that defines what normal is. But this is clearly an impossible dream. How can it be natural for a heterosexual majority to regard a homosexual minority as normal in this sense? Particularly when the gay minority goes out of its way to declare that its sexuality (which could be kept private) is its defining trait? How could anyone expect this? Even within its own birth family, the gay child is destined to be different. The heterosexual parent of a gay child can surely love that child equally with its heterosexual siblings; but can he really regard that child as "equivalent to," no different than, as normal as, a child created in his own image?

And what is the downside of this, all other things being equal? I cannot see it as being very significant at all. Only slightly greater than the status of the Jews as an abnormal group in a majority Christian culture. Perhaps the gay community can learn something from the Jews. Perhaps it is the gay community that needs to accept itself as an "abnormal" group within the culture of the heterosexual majority. That would help gays to recognize the two-sided nature of the problem. Perhaps they would then understand that gays need to respect heterosexuals and their culture too.

AIDS is Just Beginning

Fourteen years and more than three hundred thousand deaths ago, Peter Collier and I wrote an early story about the AIDS epidemic in the city of San Francisco.† At the time the virus had not yet been isolated and there had been only three thousand fatalities nationally. But it was already clear to the medical community that the culprit was a retrovirus, that there might never be a cure, that AIDS cases among gays were doubling every six months, and that if the behavioral patterns of gays and drug users did not change, there would be more than three hundred thousand people dead by 1997.

In normal circumstances, the minimal public health response to an epidemic would have been to identify the carriers of the disease by mandatory testing of at-risk communities, to reduce breeding sites of the epidemic by closing gay bathhouses and sex shops, and drug "shooting galleries," and to warn those in the path of the epidemic by contact-tracing and truthful public education about the dangers of promiscuous anal sex among gays and needle sharing among drug addicts. But what Collier and I found was that none of these measures was acceptable to a powerful lobby of gay activists who were intent on establishing a politically correct third rail for public officials whose responsibility it was to deal with the epidemic. These standard public health responses were labeled "discriminatory" and "homophobic" in a campaign whose success was so far-ranging that public health officials who proposed them did so at the peril of their careers. In a shameful dereliction of duty, doctors and epidemiologists at the highest of levels of government, including the much-praised Surgeon General C. Everett Koop, have failed to raise public health issues that could have affected the survival chances of hundreds of thousands of Americans. During

---

† "AIDS: The Origins of a Political Epidemic" *Deconstructing the Left*, Second Thoughts Books, 1995.

the entire course of the epidemic there has not been a serious public discussion of testing or contact-tracing, or truthful public AIDS education for at-risk populations.

As a result of the political third rail erected by gay activists, none of the standard public health measures was ever deployed. Instead, a series of politically acceptable ideas about the epidemic and "community approved" policies for dealing with it became the only measures feasible for political leaders to advocate, for the media to promote, and for public health agencies to pursue. These ideas included a number of emotionally comfortable but medically misleading myths: that AIDS is an "equal opportunity" virus threatening heterosexuals as well as homosexuals, non-drug users along with the severely addicted; that the budget for medical research was the crucial issue in fighting the epidemic; that if science did not provide a "magic bullet" to end the epidemic, then "safe sex" with condoms and government-promoted "needle-exchanges" would.

The myths were endlessly repeated by an irresponsible press which falsely reported "explosions" of the virus in the heterosexual community, among teenagers, and among women. These misleading reports were based on statistics deceptively interpreted by the Centers for Disease Control in Atlanta, which was one of the agencies whose public health mission had been subverted early on by the AIDS lobbyists. It is true, for example, that from time to time the percentage of heterosexuals and/or women contracting the virus has increased. But this is because the gay population has been so saturated with the disease that the percentage of new cases among gays relative to the total of new cases has declined. Moreover, the heterosexuals who are infected are the wives and girlfriends (mostly black, Hispanic, and poor) of drug users, who are epidemiological "dead ends," meaning they do not by and large infect significant numbers of other heterosexuals.

A new book summarizing the epidemiological knowledge gained from nearly two decades of grim data, called *Sexual Ecology: AIDS and the Destiny of Gay Men* and written by gay journalist and activist Gabriel Rotello, finally acknowledges what Collier and I discovered at the onset of the epidemic and what other writers like Michael Fumento amplified as it progressed. Rotello's second thoughts were prompted by his recognition that the course of recent events among the AIDS-infected and at-risk gay population has utterly refuted the fundamental premise of the authorized approach to the AIDS problem. For it is now clear that there has been no heterosexual AIDS epidemic, nor is there presently any heterosexual AIDS epidemic, nor is there any likelihood of one developing. Worse yet, the development of new drugs and the "safe sex" campaign among gays have failed to stem the tide of infection and have led instead to the emergence of a "second wave" of the epidemic among the younger gay population—a generation fully aware of the epidemic's threat to its health and survival.

Thus, a 1991 study to predict the future course of AIDS infection among gay men found that more than half of all uninfected gay males were likely to become HIV positive by age fifty-five. An equally disturbing conclusion from the accumulated AIDS data is that the epidemic will not be ended by anti-viral medical fixes. This is not only because of the nature of the HIV retrovirus, which has a greater power to mutate than any previously known microbe, but because of the history of drug interventions in combating other sexually transmitted diseases. The discovery of penicillin, which unlike current AIDS drugs is 100 percent effective, was once thought to herald the eradication of syphilis. But because it created a false sense of invulnerability, and its repeated use led to the emergence of drug-resistant strains, more than fifty years after the discovery of penicillin there are more deaths from syphilis than there were when no medical remedy existed.

There is no medical cure for AIDS, but new drug-resistant strains of the HIV virus have already been identified in Thailand, raising the specter of an even more dangerous phase of the crisis on the near horizon. In these circumstances, the only way to arrest the AIDS epidemic and prevent it from becoming a permanent feature of gay existence is the remedy available at its onset that was thwarted by resistance from the gay community: to change the behaviors that feed it. Chief among these is promiscuous sex. As the epidemiological studies show, the existence of "core groups" of aggressively promiscuous gays is the key to the epidemic's progress in the United States. The HIV virus is so difficult to transmit, that only in the presence of multiple-partner core groups can the epidemic sustain itself. But these core groups and their institutional support system—public bathhouses and sex clubs— have been defended from the outset of the epidemic by gay activists and their political allies as a "civil right." They have been defined by gay leaders as the institutions of "gay liberation." All interventions to decrease gay promiscuity, whether by public education against it or by closing the commercial sex parlors, are viewed by gay leaders as "homophobic" and violations of civil rights. As one representative gay activist, quoted by Rotello, wrote: "Gay liberation means sexual freedom. And sexual freedom means more sex, better sex, sex in the bushes, in the toilets, in the baths, sex without love, sex without harassment, sex at home, and sex in the streets." In these circumstances, it also means death.

Sexual Fanatics

Six months ago I wrote that the AIDS crisis was "just beginning." Despite—even because of—the development of anti-viral drug "cocktails" and a modestly declining death rate, the sexual promiscuity among gay males that fueled the epidemic, I wrote, was likely to increase. Now there has been an alarm bell suggesting exactly that.

According to a newly released report from the Centers for Disease Control and Prevention, studies at twenty-six VD clinics across the nation show a dramatic rise in gonorrhea among gay males—traditionally a marker for rising HIV infection rates. The cause? According to the *Los Angeles Times*: "Experts suggest that the increasing success of HIV treatment with triple-drug therapies has lulled gay men into a false sense of security that may lead to a disastrous recurrence of the AIDS increase observed in the early 1980s."

Of course, neither the *Los Angeles Times* nor any of the other mainstream media reporting these statistics has focused on the real source of the problem: the re-emergence of a bathhouse-sex club culture that fosters large cohorts of promiscuous strangers spreading the infection in urban gay centers. San Francisco, the most developed of these subcultures, has the highest gonorrhea infection rates, currently, by a wide margin. Cowed by the politically correct activists who have crippled the battle against AIDS, the media have turned a blind eye to the rash of new sex clubs and refuse to make the connection that AIDS is as much a behavioral as a clinical disease.

About the time my article appeared, a group of left-wing academics known as "queer theorists" met at the Lesbian and Gay Community Services Center at New York's City Hall. Among those present were professors Michael Warner of Rutgers and Kendall Thomas of Columbia University, living examples of how the universities routinely provide a political platform for extremists, especially sexual extremists. The group had gathered to found an organization called Sex Panic, whose agenda was twofold: First, to oppose any attempts by health authorities to curtail or restrict public anonymous sex and the institutions that support it; and second, to destroy the reputations of the handful of courageous gay activists—Gabriel Rotello, Michelangelo Signorile, Larry Kramer, and Andrew Sullivan among them—who were fed up with the homicidal sex strategies of the gay left and had the guts to publicly target them.

Warner is Sex Panic's best-known theorist. He declares himself (and all queer theorists) a militant opponent of "the regime of the normal"—a regime that includes standard public health methods for fighting epidemics. Here is Warner defending the death camps of the current contagion: "The phenomenology of a sex club encounter is an experience of world making. It's an experience of being connected not just to this person but to potentially limitless numbers of people, and that is why it's important that it be with a stranger. Sex with a stranger is like a metonym." (Warner is a professor of English literature.)

The October *Lingua Franca* describes a recent public meeting of Sex Panic at which the assembled treated with respectful silence a convicted child molester and his declaration that he was one of them. Another gay man who said that he felt the gay community's celebration of promiscuity made it more difficult for him to maintain a monogamous relationship was heckled. The flyer announcing the event was headlined "DANGER! ASSAULT! TURDZ!" The "turds" in question are Rotello, Signorile, Kramer, and Sullivan.

The author of the *Lingua Franca* article, a gay graduate student at Columbia University, could not find one queer theorist who would defend the infamous four, or who believed that shutting down sex clubs or avoiding promiscuous, anonymous sex had anything to do with battling AIDS. Instead, Warner and his fellow queer theorists proudly declare, they are opponents of "not just the normal behavior of the social, but the idea of normal behavior."

They couldn't have it any other way. Any acknowledgment of "normality" would suggest that the promotion of promiscuous sex in the midst of the AIDS epidemic is perverse at best and accessory to murder at worst. If heterosexuals were to defend gay sex clubs in the face of the AIDS epidemic, their motives would be properly suspect. Still, the silence of liberal heterosexuals, in the groves of academe, in public health departments, and in the pages of the mainstream press, lends a quiet support to this intellectual fascism and sexual fanaticism that diminishes the prospects of survival for America's gay men.

Vladimir Lenin

Angela Davis

Benito Mussolini

Andrea Dworkin

Up from Multi-Culturalism

L ike most of the destructive movements of the Twentieth Century—socialism, fascism, nihilism—multiculturalism is an invention of well-fed intellectuals. It did not well up from the immigrant communities and ethnic ghettoes of America as an expression of their cultural aspirations or communal needs. In fact its primary sponsor and most effective agency has been the Ford Foundation, a ten billion dollar tax-dodge created to protect the fortune of America's leading industrial bigot. In the 1920s Henry Ford published the *Protocols of the Elders of Zion* as a public service and influenced Adolf Hitler's anti-Semitic crusade, winning himself an Iron Cross in the process. After his death, his Foundation passed into the control of the intellectual left and its fellow-travelers, the bureaucratic mandarins and the parlor socialists of the monied elite.

In addition, multiculturalism, as we know it, would not have been possible without the catastrophe that has befallen our colleges and universities in the post Sixties era. I am referring here to the politicization of the academy and the debasement of the curriculum, the transformation of significant areas of its liberal arts program into a crude indoctrination platform and recruiting center for the America-hating, crypto-Marxist left. This intellectual plague has been described bluntly by Harold Bloom as "Stalinism without Stalin. All of the traits of the Stalinists in the 1930s, are being repeated . . . in the universities in the 1990s." I am going to make an emendation to Bloom's description a little later. The mentality *is* Stalinist, but it is the particular Stalinism of Antonio Gramsci that informs the multicultural fervor in the academy. As I will further explain, the postmodern left owes more, intellectually, to Mussolini than to Marx.

But we need to pause, first, over the fact that multiculturalism would not have been possible without the Ford Foundation and its tax-avoiding largesse. The American system of higher education in its own environment is remarkably diverse. There are more than three thousand institutions of higher learning in this country, occupying a pluralistic cultural geography. There are public and private colleges, technical institutes and schools of the arts, land-grant schools and schools with denominational affiliations, and many others besides. It is almost inconceivable that all these institutions would adopt a single party line, and would do so within the space of a decade or two, as they have on the multicultural front—and on so many other fronts dear to the left. How is this possible?

Well, it is possible if you have a pile of money, larger than the discretionary spending of the federal government in these areas, and you are viewed as a benign force by the academic community itself. The power of the Rockefeller, Carnegie, and Ford Foundations and their clones to shape America's institutions of higher learning is by no means new. At the very beginning of the era of the modern university, for example, Andrew Carnegie decided that it would be a good idea to give college teachers pensions. A college president was pretty hard-pressed to refuse such a gift, if he wanted to retain the best faculty available. Accordingly, the Carnegie Foundation attached some conditions to its grants, and it is these conditions that served to shape the entire educational era that followed.

The Carnegie Foundation began by announcing that only colleges, as defined by itself, would be eligible for the grants. The Foundation then defined a college as requiring so many hours of secondary school education (which are still known as Carnegie Units), as possessing an endowment of at least five hundred thousand dollars, as having at least eight departments, and with each department headed by a Ph.D. That was how the Ph.D. became the key to the academic kingdom. Never, of course, has there been a more conformity-creating credential. (The Ph.D. means that university intellectuals are required to beg the approval of their betters for the decade that shapes their professional life. This credentialing system has been more effective than a Central Committee in creating ideological conformity in the ivory tower.) The Carnegie Foundation also announced that it would not fund pension programs for religious institutions. That was how Brown, Drake, Wesleyan, and many other colleges gave up their denominational affiliations, and how the secularization of American higher learning began. As a congressional commission asked at the time: If a college will give up its religious affiliation for money, what will it not give up?

Since that time, the power of these elite foundations has only grown. A crucial flexing of their financial muscle, with ramifications for the present ideological of the campus, came in the 1940s in response to the Second World War. At that time, America's spy agency, the OSS, developed a need for "area specialists" for its intelligence operations. The department system that the Carnegie Foundation had created was not functional in creating intellectual specialists for military intelligence, which had more specific agendas than the "disinterested pursuit of knowledge" could service. It had no use for historians, political scientists, or economists as such. The OSS wanted specialists in the particular geographical areas and national units it had targeted for attention. For efficiency reasons it wanted these specialists to have an inter-disciplinary approach to the targets in question, a demand that the university as then constituted could not fulfill.

The solution was to reshape the university. The OSS turned to Rockefeller and later, when it became the CIA, to Ford. Grants were offered for the creation of "area studies" programs and area specialists. The Russian Institute at Columbia and the Asian Studies Center at Berkeley were prototypes of the new academic curriculum. Naturally there was powerful resistance from the conservative forces in the university, the departments, and the scholarly disciplines which regarded this as an abusive intrusion into academic concerns and a debasement of their intellectual pursuits. But just as naturally the money provided by Rockefeller and then, by Ford, overrode these objections and the new interdisciplinary area studies programs flourished in schools all over the country.

Like the spy chiefs of the Central Intelligence Agency, Marxists also favor the interdisciplinary approach. Marxism was never about "economics" but always "political economy," a theoretical agenda embracing all aspects of society and culture in the service of midwifing a new human cosmos. That is because Marxism, and all species of post-modern radicalism, are totalitarian in their ontology, their epistemology and their political agendas. Nothing escapes them. Like all gnostics, political radicals are confident that they possess the theoretical key that will unlock the mysteries of humanity and society. Of course they don't believe in any immutabilities like human nature, which in the preposterous view now proposed in the university is "socially constructed." Their agenda, like that of Lenin and Hitler, is to reconstruct the world, and to create the new men and new women who will inhabit it (and think just as they do). Such an enterprise requires an adolescent credulity, an amnesia towards the past and an interdisciplinary approach.

That is why the radicals of the Sixties, when their revolution in the streets came up empty, turned to a vulnerable, open, and essentially defenseless institution for a last act of desecration and conquest. That is why they began colonizing the university with spurious intellectual projects that looked a lot like the CIA area-studies programs. Soon there appeared black studies (now African-American of course), women's studies, queer studies, cultural studies, and even American studies, the closest clone of the CIA prototypes, targeted not on foreign adversaries, however, but on the indispensable, one might even say constitutive, enemy of the left-wing imagination—the USA itself.

What made the routine violations of academic norms and the subversion of institutional traditions possible was millions upon millions of dollars of bribes in the form of grants, subsidies and other awards to administrators, academics and institutions by the Ford Foundation and its satellite donors. It is no exaggeration to say that without the financial intervention of the Ford Foundation there would be no African-American studies, women's studies or queer studies as we know them.

What is multiculturalism? Well, in the first place, as my partner Peter Collier has pointed out, it is two lies in one word, since it is neither multi- nor cultural. It is, instead, fundamentally political and, like Stalinism, allows only one party and one party line. Its bottom-line agenda is the deconstruction of the idea of American nationality, in the service of the mindless, destructive, never-ending radical assault on the capital of the democratic world. *Because* it is the capital of the democratic world. Multiculturalism is the team banner of the hate-America left.

From its inception as a nation of immigrants two-hundred-odd years ago, America has been the most inclusive multinational, multiethnic society, unparalleled in all human history in its success in integrating diverse communities on the basis of an ideal of equality. This success has been predicated on an American culture (not a multiculture) that makes that integration possible and sustains that American idea.

Multiculturalism is a head-on challenge above all to the notion that there is an American culture and that this culture is superior to all other cultures in precisely the ambition to be inclusive and equal, and that, consequently, this culture is the very crucible of America's future and its multiethnic success.

Multiculturalism is the place the left went to lick its wounds when the Sixties were over, and to carry on its malevolent agendas. The question radicals faced at the time was: How to continue the war against the evil empire—America—now that socialism was bankrupt. You do it the Gramscian way—Antonio Gramsci being one of the many many disreputable Communists (and not a few disreputable Nazis) who have been enshrined as intellectual icons by the academic left. Gramsci's addition to Marxist theory was to suggest that by seizing control of the culture you could extend that control to the rest of the social order as well. Never mind that the notion that the ruling ideas may not be the ideas of the ruling class destroys the entire edifice of Marxist theory. Logic was never a strong point of the left. The real beauty of Gramsci's strategy is that it lets you forget about economics (which you never understood anyway) and about the colossal failure and consummate evil of actual socialist achievements, while continuing your adolescent hatred for America and its immense good works.

If you need an academic rubric under which to carry out this nihilistic attack, try "critical"—as in critical legal studies, critical race theory, or critical theory as such. Marx and his friends in the Hegelian Left were, of course, the original "critical theorists," but the ones you want to especially model yourselves after are those of the Frankfurt School—deracinated Marxists who fled to the America they hated when the Hitler radicals came to power. Much earlier than you, Adorno and co. had lost faith in the proletariat, and in the liberated future as well. But they also did not want to give up their totalist assault on the bourgeois culture that gave them freedom to spew their abuse, and that had saved their lives as well.

Along with spiteful hatred, another socialist frisson of the multicultural moment is the postmodern view that everyone (except white people) and every culture (except Western culture) is equal, and deserves equal respect. The culture arrogantly called Western Civilization is exclusionary and has to go. *Your* canon has the imperialists, the guilty, and the white, while *ours* has the innocent, the oppressed, and the persons of color. *You* have Homer and Shakespeare, and *we* have Rigoberta Menchu. Alongside the less appetizing aspects of the academic nightmare the left has created, its capacity for self-parody is almost endearing.

In locating the roots of multiculturalism, we have to take into account a second catastrophe, in addition to the one that has befallen the academy. This is the catastrophe of the left itself. Over the last several decades, even as the star of the left has ascended in the academic firmament, it has become obvious to most ordinary mortals that the intellectual tradition of the left, the tradition that currently and promiscuously embraces Marx and Foucault, Heidegger and Derrida, Angela Davis and Andrea Dworkin, Frederic Jameson and Michael Lerner, is bankrupt. Socialist economics, critical theory, and progressive loyalties have produced the worst atrocities, the most horrific suffering, the most crushing oppression, and the greatest economic misery in all human history. But not for a moment, in the nearly ten years since the fall of the Berlin Wall, has the left begun to face these failures, or confront its deeds, or figure out what are the real world consequences of its impossible dreams. It has simply moved on to another trench in its permanent war against the West—the English and Comp Lit departments of American universities. And in the course of this move, it has degenerated from a Stalinist universalism to a neo-fascist tribalism, which is what multiculturalism is really about.

There is a historical precedent for this postmodern devolution. At the time of the First World War it had also become apparent to socialists like Lenin and Mussolini that something was awry in their totalist perspectives. A funny thing had happened on the way to the war. The proletarian international was supposed to heed Marx's reminder that the workers of the world had no country, and therefore to unite in opposition to the inter-imperialist conflict. Instead, the socialist parties of Germany and France decided they had more to lose than their chains and voted to support their national bourgeoisies and the war budgets that made the conflict possible. The socialist idea had collapsed.

In response to this debacle of Marxist theory, the Left of course did not decide to do the honorable thing—pack up its bags and go home. It wanted to continue its own war against the capitalist democracies of the West. Two paths lay before it. The Leninist path held that conspiratorial vanguards were necessary to make sure that the working classes would behave as they were supposed to—in conformity with socialist theory. Lenin created the Communist International to crack the whip of theory over the huddled proletarian masses. But its human agents nonetheless stubbornly obeyed the dictates of reality rather than theory and, instead of acting as an international vanguard, quickly became an army of frontier guards for the Soviet Union.

Mussolini chose the other course. He decided that the true revolutionary agency was not an international class without property, but the nation itself. Fascism, in fact, was a socialism of the People, spelled with a capital P or, if you happened to live in Germany, with a V for *Volk*. This is the real intellectual heritage of today's post-modern, politically correct, and multicultural left.

I quote the political scientist Stephen Holmes of the University of Chicago: "Every anti-liberal argument influential today was vigorously advanced in the writings of European fascists, [including the critique of] its atomistic individualism, its myth of the pre-social individual, its scanting of the organic, its indifference to community, . . . its belief in the primacy of rights, its flight from 'the political,' its decision to give abstract procedures and rules priority over substantive values and commitments, and its hypocritical reliance on the sham of judicial neutrality."

Gene Vieth has put it more directly: "Cultural determinism, the reduction of all social relationships to issues of sheer power; the idea that one's identity is centered in one's ethnicity or race; the rejection of the concept of the individual . . . all of these ideas are direct echoes of the fascist theorists of the 1930s."

Or, to put it even more succinctly, "identity politics"—the politics of radical feminism, queer revolution and Afrocentrism—which is the basis of academic multiculturalism, is a form of intellectual fascism and, insofar as it has any politics, of political fascism as well.

Tiananmen Square
June 5, 1989

Karl Marx

atlos

Berlin Wall
November 13, 1989

Karl Marx and the Los Angeles Times

I t is the one hundred and fiftieth anniversary year since the publication of the *Communist Manifesto*. To commemorate the occasion, the *Los Angeles Times Book Review* organized a symposium of experts and asked them to assess its significance in light of all that has happened since it was written. I was one of those asked to contribute and I submitted the following two hundred and fifty-six-word article. The symposium appeared on Sunday, February 8, 1998, along with half my article:

The *Communist Manifesto* After 150 Years

The opening statement of Marx's famous *Manifesto*, that the history of mankind is the history of class struggle, is really the essence and sum of its message. This message is above all a call to arms. According to Marx, democratic societies are not really different in kind from the aristocratic and slave societies that preceded them. Like their predecessors, liberal societies are divided into classes that are "oppressed" and those who oppress them. The solution to social problems lies in a civil war that will tear society apart and create a new revolutionary world from its ruins.

This idea of Marx has proven to be as wrong as idea any ever conceived and more destructive in its consequences then any intellectual fallacy in the history of mankind. Since the *Manifesto* was written, one hundred and fifty years ago a hundred million people have been killed in its name. Between ten and twenty times that number have been condemned to lives of unnecessary misery and human squalor, deprived of the life chances afforded the most humble citizens of the industrial democracies that Marxists set out to destroy.

Marx was a brilliant intellect and a seductive stylist, and many of his insights look reasonable enough, on paper. But the evil they have wrought on those who fell under their practical sway, far outweighs any possible intellectual gain. It would be a healthy development for everyone, rich and poor alike, if future generations put Karl Marx's *Manifesto* on the same sinister shelf as *Mein Kampf* and other destructive products of the human mind.

The request for my contribution had come from the editor of the *Book Review*,

The request for my contribution had come from the editor of the *Book Review*, Steve Wasserman, an old radical friend from Berkeley. Wasserman had been a political protégé of Tom Hayden and *Los Angeles Times* correspondent, Robert Scheer, when they were leaders of the "Red Family" and were running around quoting Mao Tse-tung and Kim Il Sung, while attempting to organize "guerrilla fronts" in American cities. They hoped to launch a "war of liberation" in America, and Wasserman was one of their foot soldiers. Inspired by texts like the *Manifesto*, the Red Family practiced with weapons at local firing ranges and planned for the day when they would abolish private property and smash the bourgeois state. It was therefore of some interest to me how Wasserman would treat the *Manifesto* now that he was an editor of one of the largest metropolitan newspapers in America.

After the failure of the revolutionary hopes that the Sixties encouraged, Wasserman had gone into the literary world and become the editor of Times Books, a New York publishing house, before arriving at the *Times*. I kept in touch with him from a distance over the years. Although chastened by his experience in the revolution, like many other radicals he had not given up on the intellectual traditions and political ambitions that had unleashed its destructive energies. So I was curious and interested when he called me to this task.

Wasserman requested a piece assessing the *Manifesto* in two hundred and fifty words. At two hundred and fifty-six words, the article I submitted was six over his specification. But when it came to publishing the piece, he cut the first one hundred and twenty-six words, so that the copy available to 1 million *Times'* subscribers began with the sentence in the middle paragraph that reads "Since the *Manifesto* was written one hundred and fifty years ago . . . ." The part of the article that described the sinister message of the *Manifesto* as an incitement to civil war and pointed out the falsehood of all its major claims did not appear.

Wasserman had not indicated to me his true design, which eventually required that space be taken from my piece and given to others. He had told me that the symposium would include six or seven writers, and I assumed that each would have two hundred and fifty words. Not so. The "symposium" of mini-pieces was actually appended to a two-page spread with a picture of Marx and a poem by the German Communist Bertolt Brecht. It featured a *three thousand* word essay that celebrated the wisdom and prescience of a prophetic masterpiece. This lead article was written by Eric Hobsbawm, an unreconstructed Marxist who had joined the British Communist Party in the 1920s and remained a member through the 1960s and all the slaughter of innocents along the way. Hobsbawm's worshipful paean to the Manifesto was the real impression with which the *Times'* editor wanted to leave his readers.

"actually existing socialism" and not "real socialism." Therefore, it had little to with Marx. My comments about one hundred million people being killed were obviously beside the point, even though Marxists like Hobsbawm had done the killing and had justified it to fellow travelers and credulous followers in the West. For Hobsbawm, the *Manifesto* was not really a historical document. It was a living prophecy, correctly analyzing the dynamics of capitalist societies and providing a vision of the social future. The concession Hobsbawm was willing to make was that Marx was not correct in predicting that the proletariat would be the carrier of revolutionary truth: "At the end of the millennium we must be struck by the acuteness of the Manifesto's vision of the then remote future of a massively globalized capitalism, . . ." But, "it is now evident that the bourgeoisie has not produced 'above all, its own gravediggers' in the proletariat."

The error is of no consequence, however. The *Manifesto's* central theme remains that democratic capitalism must be destroyed or it will destroy us. Even the failure of Communism only strengthens this idea, according to Hobsbawm: "The *Manifesto*—it is not the least of its remarkable qualities—is a document that envisaged failure. It hoped that the outcome of capitalist development would be 'a revolutionary reconstitution of society at large,' but, as we have already seen, it did not exclude the alternative 'common ruin.' Many years later another Marxian rephrased this as the choice between socialism and barbarity. Which of these will prevail is a question which the Twenty-first Century must be left to answer."

In other words the democratic society we inhabit, with living standards higher and living conditions better for the mass of its citizens than have been available to any other people since the beginning of time, is no more than "barbarity"—a "common ruin." And the only alternative is the socialism that Marx really envisioned.

This, in 1998, is what the editor of the *Los Angeles Times* thinks is the epitome of progressive thought and useful for his readers to believe. Of course the slogan "Socialism or Barbarism" was first raised by Rosa Luxemburg at the end of the First World War, when Communists like Hobsbawm set out to destroy the liberal societies of the West and to create a Marxist utopia in the ruins of the Russian empire. Seventy years and one hundred million deaths later, Eric Hobsbawm and Steve Wasserman have apparently learned little from the experience. Of course, neither Hobsbawm nor Wasserman is going to mount the barricades tomorrow and attempt to implement the vision laid out in this intellectual trash. But might not others, younger than they be tempted to do so? And is not the persistence of the ideas associated with the *Manifesto* a primary cause of the corrosive cynicism of the intellectual class towards private property, individual rights and the economic mar-

intellectual class towards private property, individual rights and the economic market, which are the foundations of our free society?

When the symposium appeared, I did not attempt to phone Wasserman. Instead, I wrote him a note:

February 16, 1998

Dear Steve,

The seventy fifth anniversary of *Mein Kampf* is coming up. It's too bad that Heidegger and deMan are dead, but I'm sure you could get David Irving or David Duke to come up with a three thousand word spread telling us why, even though it was written so long ago and has resulted in nothing but human misery ever since, it is still one of the most prescient and indispensable works for understanding Western Civilization and the Jews. You might also try that French Holocaust-denier, Faurisson, whom Chomsky likes so much. For my part, I'll be glad to provide you with two hundred and fifty words of balance again. Of course, if you should you need more room for the fascists, feel free to cut whatever I send you in half.

How embarrassing, my friend.

David

On March, 20, 1998, after receiving a phone call from me on another matter, Wasserman responded:

Dear David,

I would have responded immediately to your letter of 16 February had you not e-mailed it. I don't have e-mail, alas. I do reply, however, to all missives received via post or fax. Nevertheless, I am happy to have your note, however belatedly.

Let's agree to disagree. *Mein Kampf* is the rant of a madman. There is nothing in it whatever of any merit. It remains interesting only because its author went on to create (and to preside over) on of the most monstrous and murderous regimes it was humanity's misfortune to suffer.

This is not the case with Marx who never killed anyone nor ruled a state whose purpose was genocide. To be sure, ideas have consequences and much of the chiliastic impulse in Marx was deeply, profoundly dangerous. But to read history backwards, to hold him guilty for the sins of those came after him, is I believe, an error. Moreover, much of what he wrote about capital-

ism, alas, he was dead wrong.
Best wishes, as ever
Steve Wasserman

March 23, 1998

Dear Steve,

Thanks for the reply. Now I know why you felt you could cut my little piece in half, eliminating 1) my analysis of what the *Manifesto* is about and 2) my conclusion that what it had to say has been refuted, in a definitive way, by the tragic history of Marxist regimes. The reason you thought this matter was dispensable is because you not only disagree with it, but think it is a claim without merit.

"Much of what [Marx] wrote about capitalism remains as penetrating as the day he penned his polemics." Like what for instance? The labor theory of value, the reserve army of the unemployed, the rejection of the market, the reduction of political and historical issues to issues of economic class, the prediction of increasing class polarization, the prediction of increasing misery, the prediction of a falling rate profit, the prediction of capitalism's collapse? Marxism is mythology. The fact that you don't realize this yet, is not a satisfactory reason for censoring the views of those who do.

Your desire to hold Marx, and Marxists like Hobsbawm, blameless for the deaths of millions is touching but not very persuasive. The view that Marx was right about capitalism but wrong about socialism is superficial in the extreme. The entire Marxist critique of capitalism is premised on the assumption that a socialist economy is possible. Von Mises and Hayek refuted this assumption theoretically seventy years ago. The history of those seventy years has proved socialism impossible in practice. There is nothing significant left of the Marxist analysis after this. My problem with your editing of the symposium is that you did not give those who have been vindicated by this awful history even a chance to make this case, while you gave those like Hobsbawm, with blood on their hands, a platform to repeat and perpetuate the errors that Marx made.

And they are not just errors. The *Manifesto*, as I wrote in the part you cut, is not only not innocent of the massacres committed in Marx's name. It is an incitement to civil war and therefore to such massacres. And you have repeated this "error" in your editing by giving Hobsbawm a platform for the same kind of incitement (although muted by an academic tone). Re-read the piece. What Hobsbawm says is that the *Manifesto* was right in its analysis of capitalism then and now, and that the choice before us is "barbarism or socialism." Read his book (*The Age Of Extremes*) and you'll find that the thesis is exactly the same. If we don't destroy American capitalism, it will destroy us. An incitement to declare war on American capitalists may not be equivalent to a call to kill the Jews, but it is not as far removed as you would have it either.

Yours,

David Horowitz

And that seems to have been the end of our correspondence on this matter.

Bill Gates

Black Panthers

Newt Gingrich

Credo

Why I'm Not a Liberal

As a man who helped to create the radical New Left in the Sixties, and who became a conservative in the Nineties, I am often asked to explain how it is possible to make such a one hundred and eighty-degree turn. I have tried to answer this in a book-length autobiography but there is a shorter answer as well, one that I think most Americans can easily understand as a result of recent political events. It is Bill Clinton, after all, who at the beginning of his first term appeared as a liberal of the left, proposing a government takeover of one-sixth of the American economy, and just before running for his second announced the "end of the era of Big Government" and "welfare as we know it." These two propositions, of course, are the pillars of Newt Gingrich's "Contract with America." Clinton has made his one hundred and eighty-degree turn because the American voters insisted on it. Many of the same American voters who once supported Big Government welfare programs now see they have failed. They have become believers in Newt Gingrich's contract, even if they don't realize it.

Here then is my short answer: I still believe in the liberation of blacks, minorities, and the poor, as I did in the 1960s. Only now I believe they must be liberated from the chains of liberalism and the welfare state—from permanent dependence on government handouts, from perverse incentives to bear children out of wedlock, from an inverted ethics that implies it is better to receive than to give, and worse—to receive without reciprocity or responsibility; and above all without work.

Liberalism teaches those who have fallen behind in the economic scramble to blame others for their failure. This attitude stimulates the juices of resentment and deprives its holders of the power to change their condition. On the racial front, liberalism insists on government-ordered preferences, thus delivering the message to minorities that they cannot compete unless the system is rigged. This reinforces the sense of group inferiority which is the essence of racism. Liberalism proposes universal double standards of intellectual, moral, and professional competence, teaching minorities that they can get away with less, and others that minorities can succeed only by the charity of their "superiors." Liberalism is a crippling philosophy for those it claims to help, and a not-so-subtle expression of racial arrogance on the part of those who implement it.

For liberals, something called "society" is the root of all evil: If a criminal strikes, "society" is the root cause of his malevolence; if a person is poor, "society" has made them so. If conservatives seek to hold anyone responsible for their condition, it is only out of a mean-spirited impulse to blame the victim. Only by ignoring the persistent forces of racism and oppression can conservatives maintain their belief that America is a society with opportunities—let alone justice—for all.

I used to believe all this, but then I discovered the Oseola McCarty principle of the conservative worldview.

Oseola McCarty is a seventy-five year old African-American cleaning woman from Mississippi, who appeared briefly in the nation's media last year. Having worked all her life in Mississippi, she had managed to accumulate enough savings to donate one hundred and fifty thousand dollars to a student scholarship program at the University of Mississippi. In short, a black woman, living in the most racist and poorest state in the Union (almost half her life under the system of segregation), can earn enough money cleaning other people's houses to save one hundred and fifty thousand dollars and give it away. If Oseola McCarty can do that, what American could not?

The example of Oseola McCarty tells us that the poverty problem in America is not about jobs and it is not about racism. Poverty is about individual failure. It is about family dysfunction, character disorder, and self-destructive behavior. That is what the achievement of Oseola McCarty means. It is no surprise that, while most self-appointed spokesmen for the black community get tongue-tied when asked if African Americans have made any gains as a result of the civil rights revolution, government set-asides, and trillions of dollars of redistributed income over the last thirty years, Oseola McCarty had no hesitation when asked the same question in stating the obvious. She said the world is a "much, much better place" than when she was a child.

And so it can be for anyone liberated from the philosophy of liberalism. The mantra of these liberated souls would be this: Spare us from the kindness of those who would cripple us with excuses for attitudes and behaviors that can only destroy us. Keep us from the charity of those who would chain us to their benevolence with lifetime handouts. Spare us the compassion of these saviors who secretly despise us, who think that we cannot compete on our merits, or live up to the moral standards they expect of themselves.

This is the creed of true equality. It just has taken me a long time to understand.

To Have and Have Not

I t is almost a decade since the fall of the Marxist empire, yet the crackpot ideas of its founder live on. The idea that wealth is a form of "social injustice," and that redistributing income is a worthy and progressive goal, is persuasive to people in government and out. This attitude is enshrined, for example, in the capital gains tax which specifically targets money earned from the creation of wealth. Marxist ideas are even insinuated into the language we speak. We refer casually to the "haves" and "have nots," as though in the beginning someone handed out life's goodies to those few and withheld them from the many. By using the word "injustice" to describe unequal wealth, we imply that one man's bounty can only be the result of another's deprivation.

Why do we speak of "haves" and "have nots?" What about the "cans" and the "can nots," the "wills and the "will nots," the "dos" and the "do nots?" Everyone can look around and see examples of each in their own lives. Although some inherit substantial wealth, it is will, intelligence, ability, energy, and desire that ultimately determine individual destinies, even those of the inheriting rich. Yet we persist in using terms that deny what we know.

And what we know in our own worlds is true of the world at large. According to a recent academic study reported in the *Public Interest* (Winter 1997), to be in the richest one percent of U. S. households, a family has to have over two million dollars in net worth. Yet, most of these families *earned* their wealth, because most of their wealth is in entrepreneurial assets, unincorporated businesses, or investment real estate. Moreover, the group of the very rich has changed from year to year, as reflected from survey data on unincorporated businesses which are the source of most of their wealth. Seventy percent of American millionaires are also first generation millionaires.

Redistributing wealth would itself be unjust, and destructive as well. Redistribution is merely using the force of the state to reach into the pockets of those who have earned money and to take that money on behalf of someone who hasn't. Socialism is theft. Not only is this not justice, it is destructive to the less fortunate. Suppose the government were to confiscate what Bill Gates "has"—all forty billion dollars of it, by a recent count—and distribute it to the homeless or the inner-city poor. We know what would happen to this wealth, because the government does just that every other week with welfare payments, taken from all of us who work and given to those who don't. What happens to the money? It disappears. Sometimes it is used to purchase alcohol and drugs that destroy the purchaser over time. Other times it may be used to purchase food and other necessities for subsistence. But in either case, it does not do what it does if Bill Gates invests it.

If Bill Gates keeps his capital, which he earned to begin with, there is a likelihood that he will invest it in ways that make the whole economy grow, create jobs that never existed before and even whole industries that didn't exist before. It will expand our horizons and extend our capabilities and provide us with conveniences and pleasures that we could not have imagined ourselves. To redistribute income by government confiscation is both a crime and a social evil. It diminishes capital and spreads waste.

But the doctrine of social redistribution is an even greater evil still because it sows resentment and distrust. When liberal enthusiasts inveigh against the 1 percent of the nation's households that own 50 percent of the wealth, it is an incitement of social resentment against the most productive members of the community. Of course there are also the undeserving rich, just as there are some deserving poor. But we can't make laws for everybody based on the bad apples in the barrel. Most people with money are busily producing more jobs and opportunities for others, and taking great risks to do it. That's why the market rewards them as it does. On the other hand, the resentment of wealth can build to catastrophic consequences as in the revolutions that created the Communist empire and spread misery over half the globe. Or it can lead to merely corrosive effects, making it more difficult for entrepreneurs to accomplish their agendas, thus slowing the improvement of conditions for all.

The idea of "social justice," as Friederich Hayek wrote long ago, is a "mirage," a social fiction of the Left. There is no entity "Society" which distributes income unfairly, and which could make the distribution "just." But the incentives available to a Bill Gates to accumulate billions resulted in a transformation of the world which has made life better for billions.

What would be accomplished by confiscating Gates' earnings and having them consumed in a matter of weeks? Better that the billions be invested in the creation of new enterprises and the expansion of old ones. That is surely the most "just" way to share the wealth.

Political Romance—A Cautionary Tale

W hen I was a literature student in college, my Shakespeare professor drew our attention to the way in which the playwright turned to romance as he grew older, writing a series of pastorals devoted to themes of redemption. According to the professor, this was a natural human progression, and he cited examples from other writers to prove his point. Youth is characterized by a hunger for information, he said; age distills what it knows in parables and returns to archetypal myths.

When Shakespeare wrote *The Tempest*, the most famous of his late romances and the very last of his plays, he was actually only forty-seven—more than a decade younger than I am now. Moreover, my own experience has been exactly the opposite of what the professor predicted.

Growing up in a progressive household in New York City (my parents were members of the Communist Party) I found myself enveloped in the vapors of a romantic myth not unlike that of Shakespeare's pastorals or the fairy tales that had been read to me as a child. In the radical romance of our political lives, the world was said to have begun in innocence only to have fallen under an evil spell that condemned its inhabitants to lives of pain and suffering. But there was also, according to the myth, a happy ending in store for all. Through the efforts of progressives like us, the spell would one day be lifted and mankind would be liberated from its travails. In the kingdom of freedom to come, there would be "social justice" and peace, harmony would prevail, and men and women would be utterly transformed.

Being at the center of a heroic myth provided the passions that fueled my youthful passage and guided me to the middle of my adult life. But then I was confronted by a reality so harsh and by consequences so inescapable, that the romance was shattered for good. A woman I knew—the mother of three children—was brutally murdered by my political comrades. Afterwards, the deed was covered up by my progressive community, who hoped, in doing so, to preserve their faith.

If this personal tragedy had remained isolated, perhaps the romance itself might have survived. But this murder was amplified and reflected in numerous others, most notably the slaughter of millions of peasants in Southeast Asia by the liberation fronts my comrades and I had aided and defended. When these liberations were complete, there were no happy endings. The injustice of the new orders was even greater than what had existed before. In retrospect, it became apparent to me that most of the violence in my lifetime had been directed by utopians like myself against those who refused to go along with our impossible dreams.

As a result of my experience, I developed, in age, an aversion to romantic myths. Instead, I was seized with a hunger for information—for the facts that would reveal the truth about the years I was a member of the heroic vanguard. The fall of the Communist empire and the recent publication of the Venona transcripts have only fed this passion. Preserved in the decoded communications between Soviet agents in America and their contacts in Moscow is the record of the reality we had denied, and whose denial made our romance possible. It turned out that we were just what our enemies had always said we were: members of a worldwide conspiracy orchestrated by a mass murderer in the Kremlin. Classmates of mine were revealed in the documents to be the children of cold-blooded killers for a tainted cause. Some of my parents' friends were exposed as spies. And all of us, it was clear, had treason in our hearts in the name of a future that would never come.

In the battle between good and evil that formed the core of our romantic myth, we had enlisted—New Left and Old alike—on the wrong side. We had set out as the proud harbingers of a progressive future. But what we had actually accomplished were deeds far worse than what we were rebelling against. The enemies we scorned—patriots defending America—turned out to be the protectors of what was decent and pragmatically good. They had even saved us from being consumed by our own crimes.

It became clear to me that the world was not going to change into anything very different or better than it had always been. There was not going to be a kingdom of freedom, where weapons were beaten into ploughshares and lions laid down with lambs. This should have been obvious to me when I set out in the first place. Otherwise how could Shakespeare, or writers even more ancient, capture in their creations a reality that we recognize and are still moved by today?

Revelations like these had a humbling effect. They took my mind off noble fantasies and forced me to focus on my ordinary existence: to see how common it was; how unheroic and peripheral; how ordinary and unredeemed. The revelations that shattered my faith allowed me, for the first time, to look at my own mortality. At the fact that I was not going to be born again in a new world. That I was going to die like everyone else, and be forgotten.

And that is when I realized what our romance was about. It was not about a future that was socially just, or about a world redeemed. It was about averting our eyes from this ordinary fact. Our romance was a shield protecting us from the terror of our common human fate. And that was why we clung to our dream so fiercely, despite all the evidence that it had failed; why we continued to believe, despite everything we knew. For who would want to confront such terror, unless forced to do so by circumstances beyond their control? Who would want to hear the voice of a future that was only calling them to their own oblivion?

And that is when I also realized that our progressive romance would go on. There would be some, like myself, who would wake from its seductive vapors under blows of great personal pain. But there would always be others, and in far greater number, who would not. A century of broken dreams and the slaughters they spawned would, in the end, teach nothing to those who had no compelling reason to hear, or who were to young to care. Least of all would it cure them of their hunger for a romance that is really a desire not to know who and what we are.

Steven Spielberg &
John Quincy Adams
(Anthony Hopkins)

Cinque (Djimon Hounsou)

Concluding Optimisms †

State of the Union

I lost a one hundred dollar bet when Bill Clinton became president in 1992, but even then I thought that his election might have some positive effects. During the preceding decades, the country had been ripped apart by political conflicts so deep as to create a schism in the cultural framework that held it together as a nation. It occurred to me that these divisions were not helped by the virtual monopoly of executive power that Republicans had exercised during most of those troubled years. The indictment of the USA as an "imperialist, racist oppressor" had begun during the Sixties, in the fever swamps of the hate-America left. But the fact that Republicans had almost continuously held the reins of state had also caused the animus of self-hatred and self-doubt to spread to the Democratic political opposition, and from thence to the American mainstream itself. America-bashing became a national pastime. It occurred to me that a Clinton presidency might provide certain means of correction by giving the less radical of these critics responsibility for the ship of state. What better way to restore their appreciation for what America truly was, measured not by the left's abstract and impossible ideals, but by the real and deeply flawed world we inhabit?

It is six years later and, as we approach the last quarter of the Clinton era, it appears that this hope may be more than merely quixotic. While congressional Republicans whine that Clinton has "stolen" their program, the salient fact is that his tenure has begun to bring Democrats back into the system they were in danger of abandoning. To take one crucial example: As recently as 1990, George Bush could only get three Democratic senators to support America's deployment of military force to the Persian Gulf to stop the aggressor, Saddam Hussein. In the years since, Clinton has regularly deployed American power abroad against Saddam and others without serious Democratic opposition, conveying the clear message that American power, in the post-Cold War era, is still the world's indispensable guarantor of peace. If that is not a restoration of American self-confidence, I don't know what might be.

There are deeper cultural signs of the era's healing effect on the radical wound the Sixties inflicted on Americans' sense of their national purpose. I will select two

---

† The following articles were written just before the Lewinsky scandal broke.

representative examples from the many available. In the last year, our greatest writer of fiction and our most creative cinematic talent produced singular works, each of which aspired to epic statements about the American condition. Appearing as they did at the end of a decade of post-modern cynicism, both works were striking in the deep and traditional reverence they shared for America's character and mission—for what we have been and who we are.

(Of course, over the same years, Clinton has squandered the credibility of American power, and greatly weakened America's military forces, not least through his encouragement of the continuing feminist assault on the military culture. But then, with Clinton, there is always a downside to the story.)

Philip Roth's novel, *An American Pastoral*, is an apocalyptic imagining of America's second civil war in the 1960s, pitting an immigrant industrialism against a post-industrial (and anti-industrial) counterculture. Steven Spielberg's *Amistad*, an historical re-creation of an episode from the dark age of American slavery, shapes itself as a metaphor for America's first Civil War. Although one is a work of hope and the other of despair, they are both profoundly linked in their common endorsement of the American experiment, and their shared belief in the vitality of the American dream.

Roth's central trope is the immigrant success story of a New Jersey Jewish family named Levov, and the assimilation of its scion, Seymour, into the American mosaic. As a testament to the family's success in merging the aspirations of the ultimate outsiders with the American dream, Seymour is known to friends and admirers as "the Swede." A star athlete and American golden boy, the Swede marries a Miss America aspirant named Dawn and has a child named Merry, completing the perfect American family. They live in the idyllic rural suburb of Old Rimrock, so small it has only one doctor and one all-purpose general store that doubles as the town post-office. Out of Old World filial obligation—the very sense of responsibility that once fueled a vibrant American ethos—the Swede gives up his aspirations to be a major league ballplayer and instead takes over the family business. The business is a glove factory, built up over three generations—a creation of devotion, discipline, craft, and thrift, so elaborately and lovingly described by Roth that it resonates as a symbol for American Enterprise itself.

Into this idyll comes the Vietnam War and the divisive passions unleashed by the Sixties. The Levovs' perfect daughter Merry, the quintessential American innocent, is suddenly metamorphosed into a radical anti-American terrorist ("for her, being an American was loathing America,") who blows up the general store and, with it, the town's only doctor. Merry's bomb destroys the Levov family and explodes its middle-class American dream: "That violent hatred of America was a

disease unto itself . . . . Three generations. All of them growing. The working. The
saving. The success. Three generations in raptures over America. Three generations
of becoming one with a people. And now with the fourth it had all come to nothing. The total vandalization of their world."

In the book's last sentences, Roth sums up: "Yes, the breach had been pound-
ed in their fortification, even out here in secure Old Rimrock, and now that it was
opened it would not be closed again. They'll never recover. Everything is against
them, everyone and everything that does not like their life. All the voices from without, condemning and rejecting their life! And what is wrong with their life? What
on earth is less reprehensible than the life of the Levovs?"

Who would have thought that the writer of *Our Gang*, an unforgiving Sixties
satire of the Nixon era, would, in 1997, deliver a paean to the America that the
Sixties destroyed, a passionate defense of the American way of life?

Spielberg's epic tells the story of the revolt of African prisoners on the *Amistad*,
a Spanish slaver, and their fight through the American court system to regain their
freedom. Coming at a time when voices on the cultural left are identifying American
slavery as a black "holocaust" in an image conjuring parallels between America and
Nazi Germany, *Amistad* goes through the heart of that darkness to remind us of our
worthier roots as a beacon of human freedom, even in those unhappy times. *Amistad*
recalls that Africans were enslaved by other Africans; that, inspired by their democratic and Christian ideals, Americans and Britains ended slavery and the slave trade
at a time when they persisted in Africa itself; and that white as well as black
Americans were willing to risk their lives for the freedom of all.

The film's moral is delivered by its charismatic hero, the African rebel Cinque,
who tells John Quincy Adams that he is inspired by the responsibility he feels as
the embodiment of all that his ancestors were and hoped to be. Adams takes this
idea as the informing metaphor of his oration to the Supreme Court in the film's
climactic confrontation. The former president reminds the Court that America is a
nation conceived in liberty and dedicated to the idea that all men are created equal.
"We are who we were," he says echoing Cinque's existential insight. If we are to be
Americans then we must be true to this ideal. If it has to take a civil war to complete the American revolution and to keep that faith, Adam says, then let's have it.

The American idea. Still powerful, after all these years.

Of course, not everybody is aware yet that the music has changed. Roth's novel,
for example, was misread by the conservative *New Criterion* as a novel about the failure of immigrant assimilation, as though it was another politically correct efflores-
cence of the cynical culture. Liberals agreed. The *New York Times'* Michiko Kakutani
listed it among the ten best books of the year, but also treated it as a novel of failed

assimilation, as though it had been written in the Fifties. *Amistad* didn't even make many of the ten best lists. Siskel and Ebert who had selected Spike Lee's anti-white epic *X* as the best picture of its year, couldn't find a place for *Amistad* on a list that included the very slight *The Full Monty*, about a bunch of unemployed males who perform a striptease to get off the dole. When deciding its Oscar nominations the Motion Picture Academy followed suit. In fairness to liberals, it should be noted that conservative critic Michael Medved made the same choices. Anecdotally, I have encountered few conservatives who have seen *Amistad*, so convinced are they that it is bound to be one more ritual flaying of the usual suspect, white America.

But then, cultural artifacts aside, how many political pundits, besides the reviled Dick Morris, have understood the real nature of the bridge to the Twenty-first Century that William Jefferson Clinton—with or without conscious intent—may be building?

Conservatism With A Heart

Recently, the *Weekly Standard* ran a cover symposium titled "Is There a Worldwide Conservative Crackup?" The editors framed the discussion with a paradox: Conservative ideas appear to be ascendant, but the parties that represent them are getting battered. It has become the topic of the season on the political right. In a follow-up editorial page essay in the *Wall Street Journal*, two of the right's most articulate theorists, William Kristol and David Brooks, ask "What Ails Conservatism?" Their answer may be taken as an indication of the current conservative confusion.

Kristol and Brooks begin by re-casting the question in less sensational, more useful terms: "The era of big government may be over, but a new era of conservative governance hasn't yet begun. Why the delay?" Which is another way of asking why conservatives, having won the ideological war, have been unable to establish themselves as the majority party. By way of answering the question they identify three "tendencies" in the conservative movement. These are 1) the anti-government, "leave us alone" sentiment; 2) the family values current, which wants to "re-moralize" society; and 3) the federalists, who want to devolve power back to the states. What's missing in these agendas, according to the authors, is—America itself. The existing attitudes that make up conservatism, in their view, are healthy responses to the threat from the Left, but "they are insufficient without the ambitions and endeavors of a conservatism committed to national greatness . . . . Let [President] Clinton talk about building a bridge to a multi-cultural, diverse and politically correct Twenty-first Century. Conservatives should act to shape the next century as an American century."

It's not hard to see why Republicans remain the minority party. What additional constituency do these authors think Republicans would attract if they came out as patriotic nationalists and sounded the theme of American greatness more often? Because everyone presumes that Republicans are patriotic and the fact is that they do sound the theme of American greatness often. And—this is the real kicker—so does Bill Clinton.

Moreover, Bill Clinton is not silent on the other themes either. "The era of big government is over" is a Bill Clinton tag line from the pre-election State of the Union. Family values was the saccharin mantra of the Democratic convention that launched Clinton's last victorious campaign. In his acceptance speech Clinton actually claimed credit for six of the ten points of Newt Gingrich's Contract With America. And that's the point the conservative symposiasts seem to be missing: The answer to the question conservatives are asking has already been provided by the Great Antagonist himself. It is Clinton who is presiding over the conservative agenda: balancing the national budget, reforming the welfare system, toughening government attitudes towards crime, while shrinking the liberal state. Forget that in the fine print he may be undoing even as he is doing. In politics it's the perception that counts. As far as the American public is concerned this is Bill Clinton's agenda. With one crucial addition. For, in reviving his political fortunes and making himself an ascendant American leader, Bill Clinton has already shown exactly what a conservative party must look like to win the center and thus a majority of the American electorate. The secret of Bill Clinton's success is in presenting himself as a conservative with a heart.

What ails conservatives is not that people think they lack a nationalist ambition, but that they appear to have a mean spirit. In the way they present themselves, Republicans look like accountants whose principal concern is marginal tax rates, not the real human beings who make up the majority they are trying to win. What do Republicans care about? The country is distressed about declining schools, drugs, an abusive popular culture, sexual predators on the loose. Meanwhile, Republicans are busy debating whether there should be a flat-tax, a value-added tax, or a tax credit—or an emphasis on national greatness.

Republicans need to ask themselves why the American people want Bill Clinton to administer their policies—fiscal responsibility, welfare reform, law and order. It is because—however strange this may sound—they trust Bill Clinton to do it with compassion. And why do they trust him? Because they see Bill Clinton and the Democratic Party constantly identifying themselves with America's diverse constituencies, with its multiethnic and multicultural communities, and with its citizens who are disadvantaged and poor.

There is injustice in this perception. It is the liberal welfare state created by the Democrats that has destroyed the inner city family and created a culture of poverty that has blighted the lives of tens of millions of innocent children. It is liberal policies on crime that have made our nation's once safe streets a minefield of terrors for women and the young, especially in our poorer neighborhoods. It is the feel-good, relativist, anti-authority, multicultural fashions of the progressive Left that have brought America's schools to their lowest ebb in the nation's history, depriving immigrant children and the poor (who lack the means of their liberal betters to gain access to private educations) of the golden opportunity this country offers.

Now that would make a promising Republican platform: Liberate minorities and the poor, and the American people, from the chains of liberalism and the welfare state. But to be credible in advancing this agenda, conservatives have to first reach out to these constituencies, take up their cause, and show people they care.

Index

David Horowitz

is president of the Center for the Study of Popular Culture and co-editor of *Heterodoxy* and the Center's new online magazine *FrontPage* (**www.cspc.org**).

He is author of *Radical Son: A Generational Odyssey* and the forthcoming *Politics of Bad Faith: The Radical Assault on America's Future* (The Free Press). With Peter Collier he is co-author of *Destructive Generation* and *Deconstructing the Left* and best-selling biographies of prominent American families, *The Rockefellers: An American Dynasty*, *The Kennedys: An American Drama*, *The Fords: An American Epic*, and *The Roosevelts: An American Saga*.